ANNUAL 2020

1 3 5 7 9 10 8 6 4 2

BBC Books, an imprint of Ebury Publishing
20 Vauxhall Bridge Road,
London SW1V 2SA

BBC Books is part of the Penguin Random House group of companies whose addresses can be
found at global.penguinrandomhouse.com

Copyright © Woodland Books 2019
Text by Alison Maloney
Cover design: Two Associates
Book design: Clarkevanmeurs Design

Alison Maloney has asserted her right to be identified as the author of this Work in accordance with
the Copyright, Designs and Patents Act 1988

This book is published to accompany the television series
Strictly Come Dancing first broadcast on BBC One in 2019.

Executive Producer: Sarah James
Executive Producer: Leanne Witcoop
Series Director: Nikki Parsons
Series Producer: Lee English
Series Producer: Jack Gledhill
Series Editor: Robin Lee-Perrella

With thanks to: Tessa Beckett, Selena Harvey, Claire Hore, Eve Winstanley

First published by BBC Books in 2019

www.penguin.co.uk

A CIP catalogue record for this book is available from the British Library

ISBN 9781785944703

Printed and bound in Italy by Elcograf S.p.A

Penguin Random House is committed to a sustainable future for our
business, our readers and our planet. This book is made from
Forest Stewardship Council® certified paper.

Picture credits: Ray Burmiston/BBC © pages 2, 7, 9, 13, 14, 21, 23, 24, 29, 30, 35, 37, 38,
45, 46, 55, 56, 61, 63, 64, 69, 70, 75, 76, 83, 84, 87, 89, 90, 97, 98, 102, 103, 105, 106,
109, 111, 112, 117, 118, 122, 124, 126; BBC © pages 11, 33, 67, 79, 80; Lisa Davey © pages
16–17, hair by Anna Winderburn, 18–19, hair by Lisa Davey; Phil McIntyre Live Ltd © pages
51–53; Kieron McCarron/BBC © pages 26, 40, 101; David Oldham/BBC © pages 49, 73

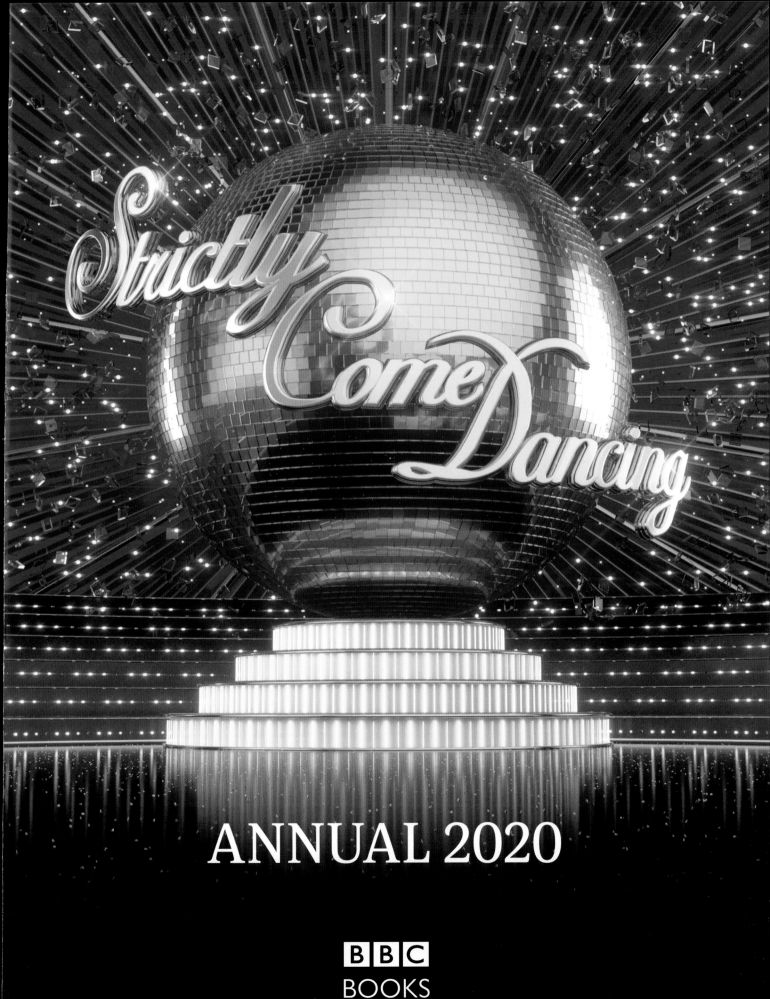

ANNUAL 2020

BBC

BOOKS

Contents

Meet Motsi Mabuse

Growing up in South Africa, new judge Motsi Mabuse was a straight-A student. But she changed her career plans after falling in love with dance – thanks to Whitney Houston.

'As a little girl, I saw Whitney performing the song "How Will I Know?"' she explains. 'I just saw her dancing, the hair and the costume, and I thought, "Wow, what a queen!" That moved me, and I always wanted to perform that way.'

In the late 1990s, South Africa saw a huge boom in ballroom, but when Motsi and her sister – Strictly's Oti Mabuse – were growing up, they struggled to find a class.

'It was a very difficult time in South Africa, so to be a little girl and push yourself in this type of dancing, where there are no other black girls, was really tough,' says Motsi. 'Even finding people to give us the instructions on how to dance was difficult, and when we did get the chance to learn the Waltz and the Cha-cha-cha, at a weekend club, we were soon better than the teacher.

'Our parents made a lot of sacrifices, because dancing is not the cheapest sport. The dresses are expensive, so my mum learned to sew, and she started a catering company to pay for the lessons and the travel abroad for competitions. They also tried to keep us grounded, because we were little girls on fire who loved dancing, but other things are important, too – like school!'

The sacrifices paid off. In 1998, at the age of 17, Motsi was finalist in the National Latin Championships, and a year later she made it to Blackpool. She then moved to Germany, where, in 2013, she became national champion with her Ukrainian partner Evgenij

Voznyuk – whom she married in 2017.

'I always said, if I'm going dance, I don't want to be just a number that nobody will remember,' she says. 'It was very important for me to leave a footprint on the planet, and when I got the German championship that was a great moment, because it was the summit of my career. I never thought it would happen and it took a lot of nerves and a lot of hard work on my part.'

Motsi went on to become a pro dancer on *Let's Dance*, Germany's *Strictly*, before taking a seat at the judges' desk in 2011. Now she's looking forward to bringing her considerable expertise to the UK panel.

'I'm so excited,' she says. 'I can't believe this is happening. It's beautiful. I know most of the dancers and I'm really happy and thankful that I'm joining the family, because everybody's so close. It's such a positive vibe.

'*Strictly* is huge. It's so glamorous. It's so sparkly. I'm a lucky girl to be part of this.'

What sort of judge are you?

My dancing career gives me an insight into how people feel when they are standing there, how they feel when they are working on a routine all week, how they feel when they perform. That helps me as a judge to choose my words carefully and to find a way to be critical but also encouraging.

How will you fit in with your fellow judges?

I have a different background and a different energy. We're all different generations and everybody's bringing something that is unique to them. We come together to form a whole that will help the celebrities get even better. I come from the ballroom and Latin world and I started my career on a different continent, which makes me see dancing from a different perspective.

What do you want to see from the contestants?

They've got to wow me. They've got to make me want to jump on the dance floor and dance myself. For me, dancing is about emotion. Dance is about expressing yourself, being authentic and showing who you are. You need to make me feel like I'm alive, and watching a dance should put fire in my belly. So I want to see the celebrities going 100 per cent. It's about energy.

What are your favourite dances?

I absolutely love the Rumba, which is my favourite Latin dance, and the Tango. They have such strong character. And it makes it a little bit easier for the celebrity to understand the dance, because they have a clear idea of character, what the dance is supposed to be about.

What is your favourite thing about the British show?

There are so many different things! I love the build-up to Blackpool, how everybody gets excited about that. I love the dance-off, because it gives everybody a second chance to really save themselves, and the absolute highlight for me is always the opening dance. I could watch them for hours, because the dancers put in so much and they get to show what they can do with their talents.

What previous dances have stood out for you?

I loved the Paso from Kevin Clifton and Susan Calman. I absolutely adored Ore Oduba's final showdance with Joanne Clifton, when they were hopping on the drums. That was so beautiful. All the pros are incredibly creative with the choreography.

Do you have your eye on anyone?

There are some athletes in there and because they have such a strong work ethic, they get along fine, although their bodies are sometimes a little bit restricted. Comedians can do well, too, because they don't mind letting go and they don't take themselves so seriously. That can be a bonus.

Which weeks are you most looking forward to?

I'm looking forward to Blackpool, because we all get to go together as a whole team, with the whole crew, and that's exciting, and I'm looking forward to Halloween, because I love the costumes and I need to have that make-up!

Stacey Dooley

Stacey Dooley was a dance novice when she first stepped onto the *Strictly* dance floor and says she was 'quite clumsy and all over the shop'. So she was stunned when she and dance partner Kevin Clifton were crowned the series 16 winners, pipping Faye Tozer, Ashley Roberts and Joe Sugg to the post in the Final.

'You never allow yourself to imagine that you could win,' she says. It was a genuine shock when I heard my name. It was an incredible moment. We'd all been dancing for months and had tried really hard and we all had the most amazing time. To win the trophy was just the icing on the cake.'

Documentary maker Stacey got off to a good start with a steady score of 26 for her week-one Quickstep and suffered a minor setback in week two – when her Cha-cha-cha scored 20. But it didn't take long for Stacey to get back in the groove.

'I still can't watch the Cha-cha-cha back!' she laughs. 'I got a 4 from Craig and it still makes me cringe. I loved our week-three Jive, dressed as the *Despicable Me* minions, and all the kids at home seemed to enjoy that. Then came our Foxtrot, which I loved. As the weeks go by, inevitably, you get a bit better.

'At the start my main goal was not to go out first. But then I realised that the public really love a trier, somebody they can get behind, so I began to think, "Maybe."'

Ever the hard worker, Stacey threw herself into the challenge, training 14 hours a day to hone her footwork.

'There were so many brilliant dancers on the show, so we had to put the extra work in,' she says. 'It is all-consuming, but you get so much support from people watching at home that you don't want to let them down. Also, because Kevin had been in the Final four

times without winning, I really wanted him to do well.

'The training is exhausting, but it's a lovely exhausted feeling because you feel like you've achieved something and learned so much.

Stacey sprang to fame in 2007 when she was spotted in a documentary about Luton airport, where she worked as a shop assistant, and was asked to front a report on the sweatshops in the fashion industry. Since then she has travelled the world, investigating issues from homelessness and women's prisons to the war in Syria.

Strictly, she says, has allowed her to show her fun side. 'Work is really intense and really serious, and rightly so, but it's lovely to just take time out for yourself and enjoy the lighter side of life. It's an amazing experience and I loved every minute.'

TV presenter Anneka Rice was so determined not to leak the news of her *Strictly* sign up that she didn't even tell her three sons – who only found out when it was officially announced.

'They're absolutely stunned because for years I've said no,' says Anneka. 'I was so worried about talking about it to my family so I just didn't talk about it. But they've been so supportive and enthusiastic.'

Born in Wales and raised in Surrey, Anneka began her career as a trainee on the BBC World Service and shot to fame as the 'skyrunner' in BBC2's *Treasure Hunt*, in 1982. Seven years later she devised the format for her own show, *Challenge Anneka*, which ran for six years and spawned a US version, hosted by Erin Brockovich, which she produced. After taking a break from TV to raise her children, she spent five years studying painting at the Chelsea School of Art.

Now her boys are grown up, the TV star has decided it's time to 'Challenge Anneka' again.

'My third son has just left university and therefore I feel a great release of mothering duties,' she says. 'It's made me feel a bit reckless this year. I've decided to be an opsimath, someone who takes up new challenges in later life.

'Earlier this year I did stand-up comedy for the first time and I painted a portrait for the Sky Arts Portrait of the Year Competition, having never painted a head before. So when the call came for *Strictly*, I thought I'd at least go and have a discussion about it. Somehow I have just been swept into the whole thing.'

Although Anneka says she loves watching dance she has never danced herself – even at family weddings.

'My son thinks I have a complete psychological barrier to dancing,' she says. 'It started when I was about seven, I was sent home from my ballet lesson because I didn't fit in with the sugar plum fairy line up which everybody else was doing beautifully. It made me feel humiliated and I never moved on from that.

'I'm a natural tomboy. I played with the kids in the street and was in the football and cricket teams at school. I knew more about the offside rule than any ballet position. My life just continued in that vein – climbing trees, playing with toy trucks, the rest is history!'

Swapping her famous jumpsuit for *Strictly* style will also be a big leap for the adventurous presenter.

'That bit slightly scares me,' she admits. 'No-one at work has ever seen me in anything but jeans so the dressing up bit is alarming. I can't imagine myself in a long dress at all. I only wore pink for the first time last Christmas.'

'I just don't know what the feminine Anneka is going to be like because every job I have done has involved me putting on a hard hat or a flying suit.'

Anneka says dance partner Kevin Clifton will need to be patient and understanding and have a 'stonking sense of humour' in training, as she is starting from scratch.

I'm so out of my depth, I feel like I've walked into the wrong film set. It's so surreal, but also very exciting!'

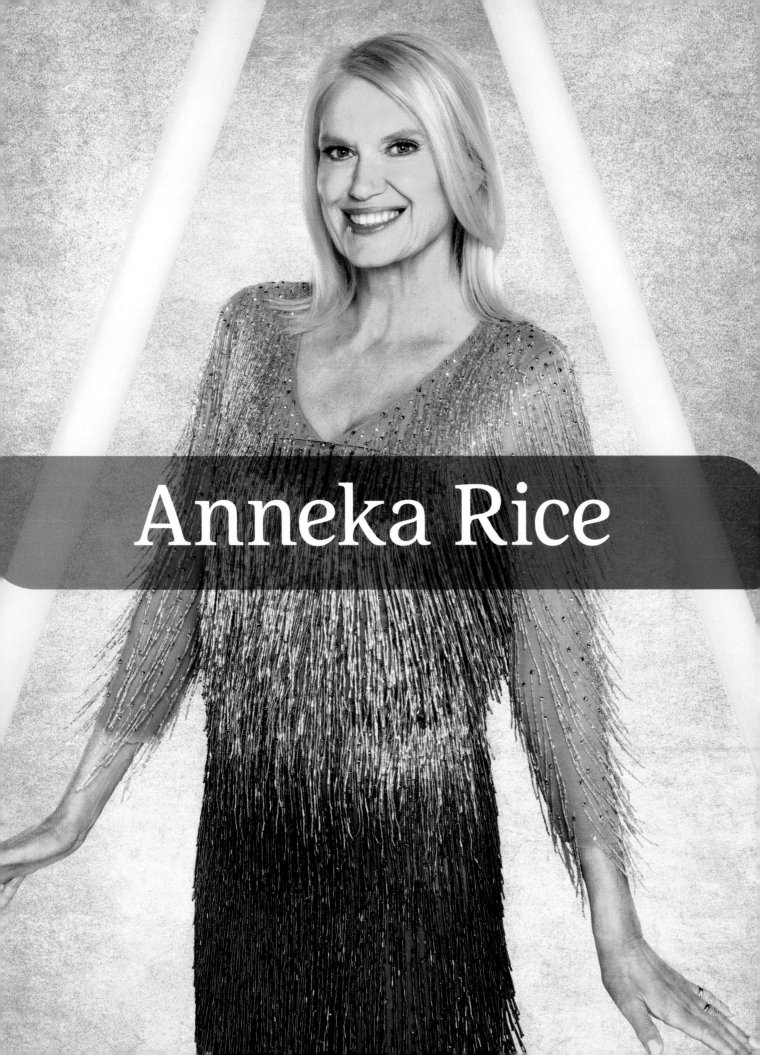

Anneka Rice

Kevin Clifton

Current champ Kevin Clifton lifted the trophy with Stacey Dooley last series, after finishing as finalist in four previous Finals. This year, he's on the hunt for more treasure with presenter Anneka Rice

'Like Stacey, Anneka has never danced before, but I think she's going to surprise people,' he says. 'She's thrown herself into training and I think, once she puts her mind to it, she's capable of good things.'

'She is really enjoying it. Anneka's giving it a good go, taking on board everything. She's got quite an analytical brain, she wants me to break it down and she's interested in all the technical elements.'

Kevin promises to get off to a flying start – with a nod to Anneka's famous *Treasure Hunt* series.

'There would be an outcry if we didn't get Anneka in a jumpsuit, leaping out of a helicopter at some point,' he jokes. 'Why not? It's *Strictly*!'

As the son of former World Champions, Grimsby lad Kevin has dancing in his blood and trained in Latin and ballroom from a young age at his parents' school. Partnered with sister Joanne, he became Youth World Number One before going on to win four British Latin Championship and International Open titles around the world, including Japan, Singapore, Slovenia and Finland.

Since joining *Strictly* in 2013, Kevin has made the Final four times, but making the winner's podium last year was an emotional moment. 'I have to admit, when we won, I was overwhelmed.

'We honestly didn't expect it, we just wanted to do our best and enjoy ourselves.

'Normally, while waiting for the result in the Finals, I'm really nervous, with a pounding heart, but that was the most calm I've been.

When Tess said our names, it was just complete shock. I was trying to hold myself together but my legs just gave way and I fell to the floor. It was a beautiful night.'

After his epic victory, Kevin put his well-earned trophy in pride of place.

'I went home, put the glitterball on the bedside table and sat in bed having a cup of tea,' he says. 'The trophy hasn't moved since, so it's the first thing I see every morning and the last thing I see at night!'

Latin Looks & Ballroom Beauty

Each dance in *Strictly* comes with its own style, and once the wardrobe department have worked their magic it's up to the hair and make-up team to complete the look. From a passionate Paso Doble to a soft, elegant Waltz, the artistry of stylists Lisa Armstrong and Lisa Davey ensures that every dancer looks the part.

But the world class *Strictly* looks don't have to just be confined to the studio. Here, the hair and make-up supremos share step-by-step instructions on how to achieve two memorable looks from Series 16.

Latin – Faye Tozer's Paso Doble

Lisa Armstrong says: 'You can tell this is a Paso look straight away. It is such a strong image. At *Strictly*, the design of the make-up has to fit the dance, and this reflects the drama of the Paso Doble through strong, heavy make-up.

'With this look, the main focus is on the eye, because a lot of the interpretation of the dance is in the facial expression. The strength, the determination and the power come through the face and the eyes.'

GET THE LOOK

STEP 1

We start with the eye make-up on a strong look like this, because there's a lot of droppage from the eyeshadow application. Prep with an eyeshadow base, which holds colour and maintains the strength of the black. Next, apply a black eyeshadow on the eyelid and blend into the crease of the eye. Then wing out to get that feline flick. Apply a line of black powder underneath the eye and sweep up into that line.

STEP 2

The line of black crystals – glued on with eyelash glue – add even more prominence to the flick. Take each crystal, add a dab of eyelash glue to the back, wait for ten seconds, then give a little blow on the back so the glue goes slightly tacky. Then apply the biggest stone to the outer corner and dot the rest, in diminishing size, along the winged line.

STEP 3

Fill in the eyebrows with a strong colour to give a structure to the eyes and add highlighter underneath the brow bone to really give it that wow effect. This look is all about the angle – so the eyebrow is really structured, the highlighter is structured, and the shape of the shadow is emphasised by the crystals.

STEP 4

Keep the skin nice and clean with a light foundation. Sweep a highlighter across the top of the cheeks and up towards the hairline, following the shape of the black flick. Add a contour underneath the highlighter.

STEP 5

Choose a matte lipstick that is not too strong in colour and not too glossy, to keep the emphasis on the eye. Line the lips with a corresponding liner and fill in with the lipstick.

STEP 6

Apply a big lash to make the eyes pop even more.

Hair

'On *Strictly* we use a lot of hairpieces to add length or thickness, and also because it makes changing hairstyles much quicker,' says Lisa Davey. 'On the day of the live show, prep is key. At the beginning of the day, we spend a lot of time prepping the hairpieces on a block. Then, once we've got our initial shape on the celebrity, we can clip them in to create the look.'

GET THE LOOK

STEP 1

Prep the hairpieces. Take a full set of eight clip-in hair extensions and make into plaits and fishtail braids, which uses the same method as the plait but with two strands instead of three.

STEP 2

For the flowing mane at the back, use your own hair (if long enough) or long hair extensions. Add texture by using a large waver, like a beach waver, for that soft wave.

STEP 3

Slick back the side section of the hair into a ponytail, and secure with a hairband. Take sections of the top of the hair, crimp the roots and backcomb to add shape and height. Then add mattifying powder and shape, securing with hairpins and then a lot of hairspray to keep in place.

STEP 4

Clip in the fishtails along the front hairline and round to the sides. Then add a long extension at the back (if using), adding grips to keep it in place. Then clip in the extra fishtails to hang at the back. Add accessories such as feathers, chain, slides – whatever takes your fancy!

Ballroom – Ashley Roberts' Quickstep

Lisa Armstrong says: 'The Quickstep is a light, happy dance, bouncy, jumpy and fun. The hair is styled so that when Ashley moves along, the hair will bob along with her. The hair and make-up is an extension of the dance, along with the costume and choreography.

'This is a completely different look to the Paso Doble. The eye make-up is really soft and blended, but it's still prominent, so her eyes still pop.

'To make it work with the bright costume, we added a splash of colour on the lip, using matte lipstick. We never use a heavy gloss for a dance like this because we want to avoid the hair to sticking to the lip gloss.

'Normally in the make-up rules, you are told, "Don't do a heavy eye with a heavy lip," but with this look it completely works because neither the eye make-up or lip colour is too strong, so it's working as a whole. This is a pretty girl-next-door kind of look. It's happy, it's lively, it's bubbly.'

GET THE LOOK

STEP 1

This look uses three different eyeshadow shades, in bronzes and brown. Start with a flat base of brown eyeshadow across the lid, then blend with a darker colour from the outer corner into the socket line to add depth. Apply the shimmering bronze to the inner corners, and under the eye.

STEP 2

Use a black liner along the inside of the lower lid. Then apply a gel liner across the lash line of the upper lid so that the lash line, the eyelash and the eyeshadow blend into one.

STEP 3

Use the lighter, shimmery bronze colour to highlight the inner corner and underneath the eye.

STEP 4

Fill in the eyebrows and add a little bit of highlighter on the brow bone and over the top of the cheek. With a pale blusher, add a pop of colour on the cheek. Then even out the skin tone with a light foundation.

STEP 5

Line the lips with a pink liner and apply a nice, bright, matte lipstick in pink. Add a fluffy lash.

LISA'S TOP TIP

'This is a little trick we use a lot on *Strictly* to accentuate the bow of the lip. Dab a little highlighter on to the back of your middle finger, tap it on to the tip of the nose and down onto the bow of the lip.

To accentuate the eyes, press the finger in the highlighter, blow off the excess and then tap it into the inner corner of the eye. It makes the eyes pop and brings structure to the nose.'

Hair

Lisa Davey says: 'For Ashley's Quickstep we wanted a classic Hollywood wave, which perfectly matches the bobbing action of the dance.

'Years ago, we would have set the hair with pinned curls, on a wet set, and it would have taken a lot longer. But now that we have hot tongs, we can create the look much faster, because we don't have time on the day of the show to have the dancers sitting under driers.

'We used hairpieces to add length, but if you have long hair you can easily achieve this look without them.'

GET THE LOOK

STEP 1

Start from the nape of the neck and, taking even sections of around an inch, spray with hairspray and then use a tong or conical wand to curl each individual section. Make sure you keep exactly the same wave, curling in the same direction, all the way round. When you finish the bottom layer of hair, repeat on the next level up and so on, until you reach the top.

STEP 2

When you have done the whole head, brush it through – as long as your curls are consistent, you'll start to get that wave. Then use a smaller brush or a tail comb to make the waves sharper.

STEP 3

To set the wave, take tissue paper and section clips and pin along the dents of the wave, all the way round. Then spray with hairspray and leave to set until it's time to dance.

Shirley Ballas

Shirley Ballas is warming up for her third series as head judge, and is looking forward to welcoming Motsi Mabuse to the panel.

I've known Motsi for many years' says Shirley. 'She's fun, lively, honest and she judges without fear or favour. Motsi comes with so much experience from the German show and she's been a competitive dancer. She's going to be a magnificent addition to this panel.'

Shirley, herself a champion Latin dancer before becoming a dance-circuit judge. 'I've got Bruno on my left with this amazing amount of energy and I've got Motsi on my right who has an equal abundance of energy. She will give Bruno a run for his money, that's for sure.'

What do you think of the line-up?

I think this is the most unpredictable line-up ever. I wouldn't like to predict this one at all. This is going to come down to dedication, hard work, endurance and mental capacity. I think any of them could be a winner. Any of them could make it to Blackpool, and once you get there, everyone is a winner in my book.

Which was the most surprising pairing?

Anton Du Beke and Emma Barton. I have to say I was delighted for him. Maybe this could be Anton's series.

Anyone else you have your eye on?

They all genuinely look like they have a spring in their step. At the Launch Show, I was pleasantly surprised, because they all have a sense of coordination and a real sense of fun. There's always great energy for *Strictly*, but I think this feels like there's even more energy that ever before!

Did you enjoy the Couple's Choices last year?

I enjoyed everything that was new last year on the show. The Couple's Choice brought something a little bit different. That's what I love about *Strictly*. There are always changes, which keep it fresh.

What were your favourite moments of last year?

The amazing journeys with Stacey Dooley and Joe Sugg. They showed that a non-dancer could really prevail at the end and that really warms your heart. It proves to everybody else in the country that they, too, can dance. Anybody can have a pep in their step if they try.

Rower James Cracknell is used to going for gold but when it comes to *Strictly*, he has set his sights on getting through week three – for a very good reason.

Croyde and his two sisters Kiki, 10 and Trixie, 8, are 'unsurprisingly mortified' at Dad's decision to join the show, says James. 'But then they've seen my dance floor moves too many times so I can't blame them.

'I showed them one of the videos from rehearsals and Kiki, who's quite to the point, said "Well you can get better!"'

Surrey-born James began rowing at school and won his first gold medal at 18, in the Junior World Championships. He went on to win two Olympic golds in the coxless fours in 2000 in 2004, and six World Championship golds before retiring from the sport in 2006.

But, ever up for a challenge, he took up cycling, marathon running and triathlon as well as competing in several yacht races, including one to the South Pole.

After a devastating cycling accident left him with a brain injury, in 2010, he defied doctors' expectations by taking on new sporting challenges, including the tough Yukon Arctic Ultra, in a 430 mile race in Alaska, and running the 2012 London Marathon in under three hours. In 2019, he became the oldest rower to compete in the University Boat Race, having enrolled to study for a degree at Cambridge.

While he's used to taking on new endeavours James, who is paired with Luba Mushtuk, could find getting the ballroom frame his greatest challenge yet. 'I've got to improve my posture for dancing so my homework is to stand up,' he laughs.

As an accomplished and determined athlete, James is used to putting plenty of time into training and says he'll do as many hours as it takes 'not to look like I'm dad dancing at a wedding.'

But he says the hardest thing will be accepting if he's not top of the leaderboard. 'My biggest challenge will be letting myself go, letting myself off the leash so I can show a different side of myself,' he says. 'I am giving myself permission to fail and that's a real challenge for me.'

After years of rowing, cycling and running, James is no stranger to Lycra and says he's happy to be *Strictly-fied*. 'I reckon the sequins and fake tan will be fun. I hope to surprise myself with how far I can get too – I'm there for a good time!

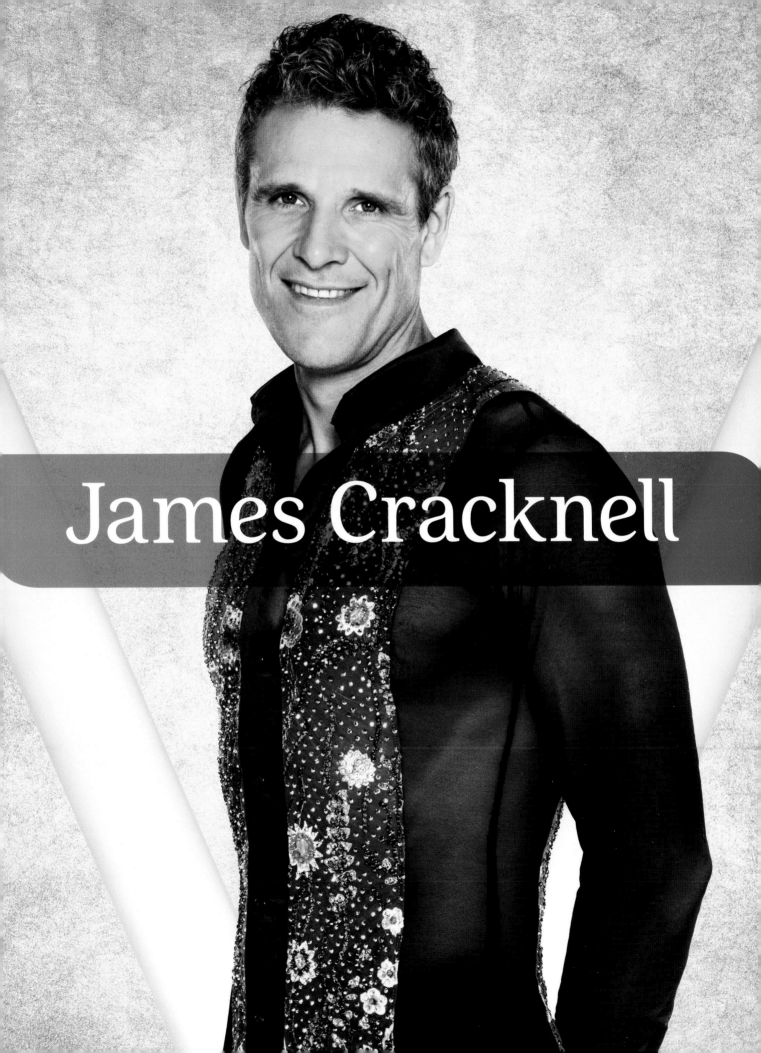

James Cracknell

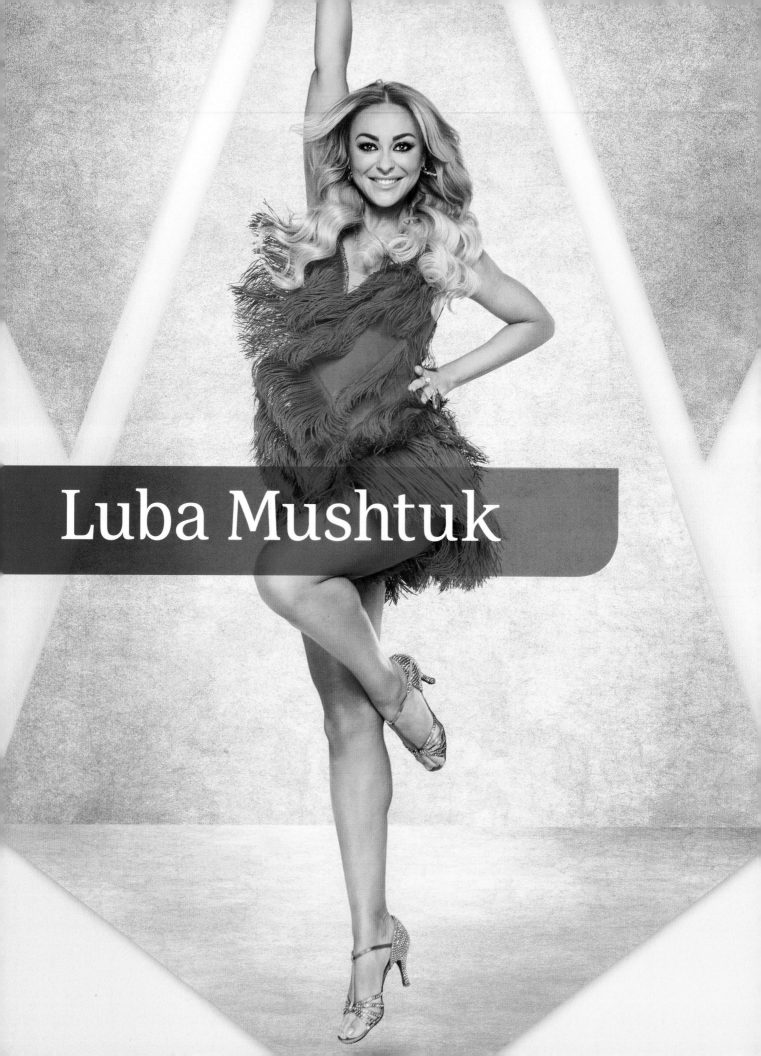

Luba Mushtuk

Although this is the second year as part of the *Strictly Come Dancing* professional team, this will be the first time Luba Mushtuk has been paired with a celebrity for the main series and she is thrilled to be dancing with rower James Cracknell.

'I'm over the moon with this opportunity to take part in this beautiful challenge,' she says. 'I'm looking forward to training and choreographing each dance. I think I've choreographed every single dance that can possibly be done by week one and I can't wait to have the songs so I can figure out how to make him look the best possible version he can be as a dancer.'

Luba was born in St Petersburg, Russia, and started competing in Latin and ballroom at the age of four. At just 12, she left home and travelled to Italy to study with 10 Dance World Champion Caterina Arzenton.

Luba became four-time winner of the Italian Dance Championship and the Italian Open Latin Show Dance champion. She was ranked second in the European 10 Dance Championships and was a finalist in the Latin European Championship, joining *Strictly* as Assistant Choreographer in 2016, and dancing on the live tour.

Luba is hoping to add another trophy to the cabinet of Olympic medalist James and thinks he could look good on the dance floor. 'It's early days but I think he could be great in ballroom because he's very tall and he has a great physique.

'This is very different from sport and none of the celebrities have ever done it before so they are all in the same boat.' As a teacher, Luba will put James through his paces. And her pupil will have plenty of input into the dances.

'I always adjust myself to the person I have in front of me when it comes to teaching and choreography,' she says. 'I will have a conversation with James and we'll see which way we want to go, whether it's more towards the entertainment part of it or more serious. Then I will do the best job to make him look the best he possibly can.'

Although this is her first series with a celebrity, Luba has already bagged herself a *Strictly* trophy.

'I danced with Shane Lynch on the Children in Need Boyzone special, which we won and that was a great experience,' she says. 'And I was paired with Jake Wood for a Christmas special which was incredible. So I still had the experience of training with a celebrity and choreographing which I really enjoyed. So instead of having one celebrity last year, I had two!'

Stuart Holdham

Every Saturday afternoon, the UK's best-dressed queue forms outside Elstree Studios as excited *Strictly* fans prepare to watch the live show. The *Strictly* fans love to sparkle so they all seize the opportunity to put on their glad rags for this very special occasion, as warm-up man Stuart Holdham can testify.

'They make a massive effort. They go out and get their hair done, get their nails done – and that's just the men,' he jokes. 'They're buying new frocks, and by the time they get to the studio, they are all looking amazing.

'Once they've got their tickets through, they have been literally counting down the days until they're there.

Then, when they are inside and seated, it's Stuart's job to entertain the studio audience before the main event. Not that they need much warming up.

'When you're in the back of the stage, where Tess and Claudia come out, you can hear the chatter, the sense of anticipation and how excited they are. Studio tickets are like the Willy Wonka Golden Ticket – the audience feel lucky to be there. Recording the show can take a long time, but you don't hear anyone complaining. If anything, they'd stay there longer if they could.'

Stuart is the first representative of the show that the live audience sees, and as well as making them laugh, he also has to deliver essential housekeeping messages.

'My first words are, "Ladies and gentleman, welcome to *Strictly Come Dancing*. Make some noise!"' he says. 'They all cheer, get it out of their system and they're attentive, and that's important, because not only do I have to tell them what's required of them, but I have to get my health-and-safety cap on and make sure they are looked after.

'I also tell them how vital they are, because they are the backbone of the show. If they didn't cheer, clap along and enjoy every dance we'd all miss the incredible atmosphere that the live studio audience create.'

As well as telling great jokes that get audience laughing and happy Stuart teases the audience with the dances they are about to see.

'They know their Latin and ballroom and they all look forward to certain dances.

Although he's now been a fixture on the set since series three, Stuart fell into warm-up by accident, while working in TV production on shows like *Blind Date* and *Ant & Dec's Saturday Night Takeaway*.

'I was working as a producer on a game show and the team had forgotten to book a warm-up act,' he says. 'I was the office joker and they said, "Why don't you do it?" It's all very well being the funny guy in the office, but doing it on stage is a different matter.

That weekend, my father, my sister and I went through every joke possible and wrote some gags down and I got through it.'

As word spread, the bookings started rolling in, and 18 months later, when the *Strictly* warm-up guy was in panto, Stuart was asked to step in. 'It was a brilliant

opportunity, which I grabbed with both hands – and I've not let go since.'

Not surprisingly, spending 14 years on the show has had a huge influence on Stuart's ever-expanding wardrobe, which now boasts 34 sparkly suits and 12 pairs of glittering shoes.

'Even Craig is pretty jealous of my wardrobe, truth be told!' he laughs. 'I have summer suits, three gold suits and three sequined suits, but my favourite suit is my LED suit, which my mother made for me. It lights up in 32 different colours and I save that for the Final. Every now and then it gives me a little jolt, but apart from that it's great. My wardrobe is now very representative of the show. It's all glitz and glamour, all eyes and teeth, all jazz hands – and that's what I give them.'

Stuart's Favourite Gags

★ Back in the day, you used to talk about facelifts and it was a taboo subject. You mention Botox today and nobody raises an eyebrow.

★ I used to be addicted to mud wrestling, but I've been clean for six months now.

★ Calendars. Their days are numbered.

★ My doctor reckons I'm paranoid. He didn't say it, but I know he's thinking it.

★ I've written a song about a tortilla . . . Well, it's more of a wrap really.

★ I'll tell you who's full of themselves, those Russian dolls . . .

Radio 1 DJ Dev Griffin is taking time out from spinning the discs to twirl on the dance floor, and he can't wait.

'When I was first asked to be a part of this year's line-up, I thought that this would definitely be one to tell the grandkids,' he says. 'I know it's going to be challenging, but it was too much of a fun opportunity to turn down.'

Dev grew up in London and attended an after-school drama club at the Anna Scher Theatre School, where he met the equally ambitious Reggie Yates. At 16, the pair landed a radio show on pirate station Freek FM, and while still studying for his A-levels, Dev moved into TV alongside Reggie, presenting the children's show Smile. The pair presented the Reg and Dev Show on 1Xtra for several years before going their separate ways, and Dev now presents the Weekend Afternoon Show on Radio 1.

During his *Strictly* run, Dev is cutting down his DJ commitments, but he says he wanted to keep some airtime open so he can share the experience with his listeners.

'Radio 1 have been incredibly supportive,' he says. 'They know I'll have to put in a lot of time in training, but one show a week will be a really nice place to decompress. It's somewhere I feel comfortable when there's a lot of stuff happening at once. It's good to have a bit of an outlet where I get to tell everybody how I feel, but also a little behind-the-scenes stuff as well.'

Although his life revolves around music, Dev has no formal dance training and is starting from scratch when it comes to Latin and ballroom.

'If you count dancing in a club with my mates, probably trying to impress a girl, then I think I'm all right,' he says. 'But actual dancing? I went to auditions when I was a kid and was surrounded by stage-school kids who were trained in ballet, tap, modern – you name it. They had all this experience and I had just danced at a few weddings.' Dev is happy to be *Strictly*-fied and rather fancies himself in top hat and tails. 'Going into the show, I thought I wanted to do all the Latin dances,' he says. 'But actually, now that I have learned some of the classier ballroom moves, I want to do that. I want to look classy.'

Planning to put as many hours as possible into training with partner Dianne Buswell, he admits he has a short attention span and may be slow to pick up the routine. But he is determined to get it right.

'People are going to be able to tell whether you're putting in the work, whether you've been paying attention. I'm genuinely looking forward to doing something I've put my mind to and seen through to the end. That might be the first time I've ever done that.' Dev says he'll be happy not to go out in the first week and to get to Blackpool – but he's cleared his diary until Christmas.

'I am fiercely competitive,' he says. 'Even if I'm not good at something and there is a competitive element involved, then I'm going for it. Whether it's the egg-and-spoon race or Monopoly, I'm playing to win!'

Dev Griffin

Dianne Buswell

Series 16 finalist Dianne Buswell is hoping it's third time lucky as she takes to the dance floor with celebrity partner number three, Dev Griffin. But she says she was surprised to be paired with the Radio 1 DJ.

'It was a shock, I didn't expect it.' she says. 'But I'm really excited about it.'

Although Dianne didn't get to dance with Dev in the opening group number, his moves didn't go unnoticed.

'He did catch my eye,' she explains. 'My task is just pulling out the dancer within. So I'm so excited to see how far I can push him. I feel like his Latin could be very natural. He doesn't have any idea about Latin or ballroom, but I feel like the Latin will really suit him. But I personally love ballroom so I'll be very strict on him in that and hopefully he'll be a good all-rounder.'

Dev has said that he wants his professional partner to be firm with him, but Dianne wants him to have fun as well.

'He told me that he's the youngest child, with three older sisters' she says. 'So he wants someone to be really strict, which I can be, especially when it comes to the dancing. But I told him he also has to enjoy the process and he needs to truly embrace every moment. It can't only be hard work – there has to be some fun. You only get this opportunity once in a lifetime so you have to have the best time possible.'

Born in Bunbury, Western Australia, Dianne began dancing at four and partnered her brother, Andrew, eventually becoming Adult New Vogue WA Champions for 2008 and 2010 and Australian Open Champions. She went on to appear on *So You Think You Can Dance Australia* and *Dancing with the Stars*.

She joined *Strictly Come Dancing* in 2017, dancing with the Rev. Richard Coles, who was third to be eliminated. Last year, she took influencer Joe Sugg all the way to the Final – a feat she hopes to repeat in series 17.

'It was absolutely amazing,' she says. 'Once you've had a taste for it, you want to be there every single year. It drives me forward to get there again. It is the best feeling ever.'

A complete novice at the start, Joe stunned judges with his Showdance, Paso Doble and Charleston in the Final and Dianne says he worked hard for his shot at the trophy. 'At the beginning, it was about banter and fun but as the competition narrowed down he realised he had a chance and he got very serious about it. We still had a good time from start to finish but I definitely saw a difference as we got closer to the final. He pushed himself harder towards the end.'

Although they missed out on the trophy, Dianne is immensely proud of Joe's huge improvement and the effect that dancing has had on him.

'To see where Joe started out and how he ended up is incredible,' she says. 'It changed his life. His confidence has grown massively. 'He's now starring in the West End which he would never have considered before *Strictly*. I always say I want my pupils to fall in love with dance, because I love it so much so, for someone to learn on *Strictly* then say, 'this is the best thing ever' is a wonderful feeling for me.'

Meet the Boss

Strictly kicks off for series 17 with a new leader at the helm as Sarah James steps up to the executive-producer role.

'I'm so proud of the show and I'm honoured to be taking over the reins,' she says. 'I'm beyond excited! *Strictly* has done so well over the last few years, so while we are moving it on all the time and keeping it fresh, we'll be sticking to the format the viewers love so much.' The Couple's Choice dances, introduced last year, have proved a hit with viewers and will return, appearing earlier in the series, and dancer Nancy Xu is joining the professional line-up.

Plus, of course, there's a new judge, as Motsi Mabuse takes Darcey Bussell's place on the panel.

'Motsi will instantly change the dynamic of the judging panel, but I really believe viewers are going to love her,' says Sarah. 'Motsi is so warm, with an amazing energy and aura, and really enthusiastic about the show. She brings something to that panel which will fit nicely with the other three personalities. And her background is in ballroom and Latin, which is great.'

There is, as always, a brand-new celebrity cast and Sarah has been working for months to put together just the right mix. 'It's an organic process,' she explains. 'Our celebrity booker Stef Aleksander starts with a long list and we meet three or four times the number of people that we actually need. It's a real jigsaw puzzle to make up a really good cast. You don't want to have 15 soap stars or 15 pop stars, so we look at a variety of ages, jobs, different personalities, dance abilities and different heights, then we whittle it down.

We hadn't cast a social-media star before last year but Joe Sugg did so well we wanted to try that again. When we met Saffron Barker, we felt she was very different from Joe but would still appeal to our younger audience.

While fans wait in eager anticipation from Christmas to autumn for the return of the show, Sarah is working all year round to make it happen.

'I start brainstorming ideas with the team in January while the last series is fresh in all our memories,' says Sarah. 'The casting process begins in February. So it starts with just me and Stef, then series producer Jack Gledhill and line producer Kate Jones come on board. We only get the full team together two weeks before the Launch Show, and that's when it starts ramping up and getting really busy. By that time, I have people queuing to ask me questions.'

Sarah began her TV career as a runner on The X Factor before working her way up to series producer. She then worked on various game shows before moving to the BBC. She joined *Strictly* five years ago.

'This is a dream job for me,' she says. 'I used to dance when I was younger, although not ballroom and Latin. I try to learn some steps from the group numbers, but I'm not quite up to the standard of the pros!'

Craig Revel Horwood

With a background in musical theatre, Craig Revel Horwood loves a bit of drama on the dance floor.

This year, Craig is hoping for something equally entertaining, and he's thrilled that the Couple's Choice category, which allows couples to choose between Street/Commercial, Contemporary and Theatre/Jazz, is back for a second year. 'I like the fact that couples can have a choice so they can build on their strengths and showcase their talents,' he says. 'It adds variety, which is important.'

Having studied the new line-up, Craig says viewers are in for a 'fantastic year'.

What do you think of the line-up?

There are some really interesting people there – I can't wait to see Michelle Visage dance. I think she's going to bring a lot of personality and give me a run for my money with some fabulous one-liners. Chris Ramsey is a great comedian and he'll bring a lot of humour to the dance floor.

I'm excited to have aristocracy on the show, in the form of Emma Weymouth. I've always said we needed royalty. I can't wait to see her in an elegant Waltz.

Who do you think may be a dance-floor hit?

Catherine Tyldesley looks like she has lovely feet, with pointed toes. I think Alex Scott has potential, because in football you have to be determined, so she's going to be strong and competitive. Karim Zeroual could also be one to watch. As a CBBC presenter, he'll be sprightly, full of energy and youth.

Who might surprise us?

I'm looking forward to watching Anneka Rice. It will be interesting to see her glammed up and wearing heels, because we're so used to seeing her in a jumpsuit, running around.

There are a few sports personalities in the mix. What are their chances?

As a rower, James Cracknell will probably have good rhythm, because the rowers all need to be in tune with each other. Goalkeepers haven't done well in the past, but let's hope David James can buck the trend. Will Bayley is a table-tennis player and they have to be fast and furious, and react very quickly, and that will be useful for dances like the Quickstep.'

What do you think of Motsi Mabuse joining the panel?

Motsi will be great. She's had nine years' experience as a judge and she's articulate. I watched some footage from Let's Dance and she looked like she knew what she was talking about – although I have no idea what she said because I don't speak German!

What would be your advice to Motsi?

Judge with both your head and your heart. And don't hand out 10s willy-nilly!

Footballer Alex Scott has a cabinet full of trophies but is aiming to add a glitterball to the collection this year. The former England ace says being asked to take part in *Strictly* already feels like putting the ball in the back of the net, though.

'I am such a fan of the show,' she reveals. 'In 2012, I tweeted a picture of me at a photoshoot in a sequinned outfit saying, "*Strictly*, I'm waiting for my call-up!" Someone pulled it out when they announced my name this year. I've been wanting to do this for so long.'

Londoner Alex joined Arsenal at the age of eight and spent most of her footballing career with the club, between stints at Birmingham City and US team Boston Breakers. In 2007, she scored the winning goal for Arsenal in the UEFA Women's World Cup and in 2012 played for England in the London Olympics. She is the second-most-capped England player, with 140 appearances, and after hanging up her boots in 2017 she became a football pundit, most recently covering the 2019 FIFA World Cup.

Despite her considerable sporting achievements, Alex says it's signing up for *Strictly* that has created the biggest reaction among friends.

'The funny thing is, I played in three World Cups and the Olympics, and when I was announced on *Strictly*, I was flooded with messages saying, "This is a dream come true for you." I never got that when I got picked for a World Cup.'

Having been out of sport for over a year, Alex says her fitness level has dropped, but she is keen to get back into intensive training.

'When I retired I wanted to get away from that mindset of being an athlete, so not training, enjoying myself and living life,'

she says. 'But it's been nice to come back to training every day. Now when friends message me, I say, "I'm off to dance today." It sounds so surreal.'

Neil Jones will be taking Alex through her paces on the show, but she has already been getting posture lessons from Oti Mabuse.

'Oti has been trying to teach me how to walk more elegantly, keeping my shoulders back,' she says. 'I'm walking around with my shoulders hunched over, so even those little tips are useful.'

Unfortunately, Alex's dazzling football career has left her with ankle injuries, but she refuses to let them hold her back.

'My biggest worry is my ankles and being in heels all the time,' she says. 'But it didn't stop me seeing out the end of my years in my football career and it won't stop me now. You've got to enjoy the moment. We're in the *Strictly* bubble, it's a once-in-a-lifetime experience and you've just got to go with it.'

In fact, the sporting heroine can't wait to swap her football strip for a glam frock. 'I want to show the other side of female sports. Yes, we are athletic, we love sports, but we also enjoy being glamorous. I love having my make-up done for me – I don't have a clue how to do it myself. But that transformation will be great. I will enjoy being that alter ego.'

As a sportswoman, Alex is fiercely competitive and is definitely in it to win it.

'I've always wanted to be a part of this, so I will be devastated if I go home early on and I end up watching later rounds from my sofa,' she says. 'I just really don't want it to end too early.'

But learning to dance is her main goal. 'I want to move on from the two-step when I go out with the girls. I want it to be so, when a song comes on, I can say, "I've got this." Imagine having that moment!'

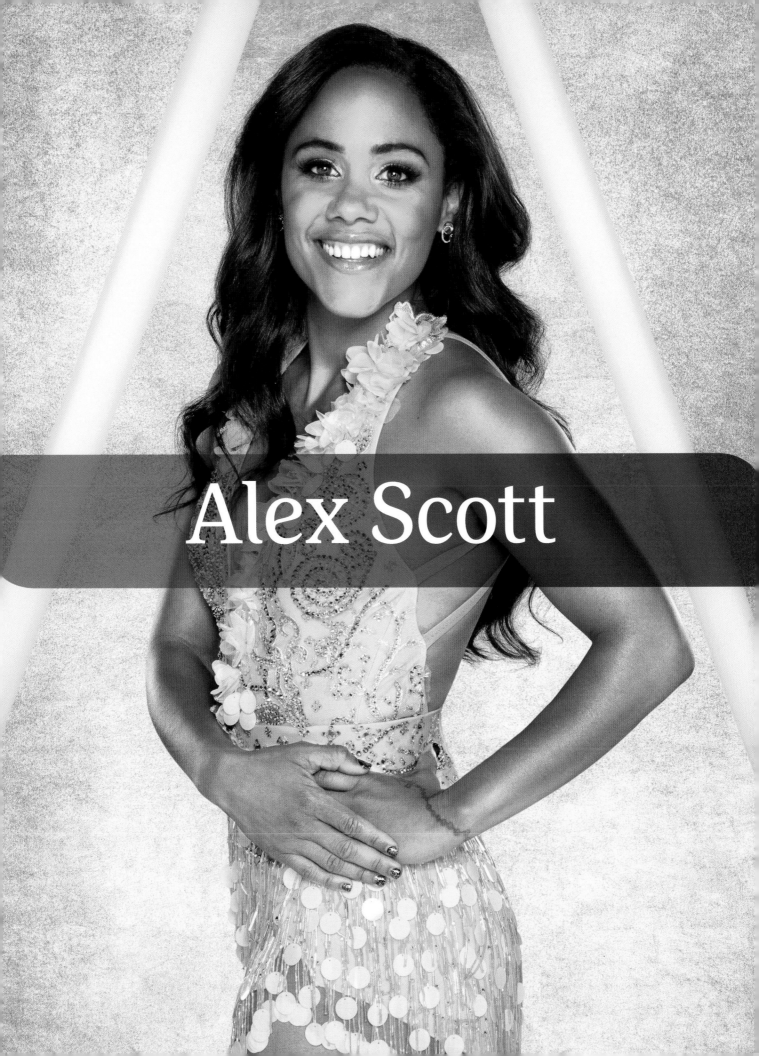

Alex Scott

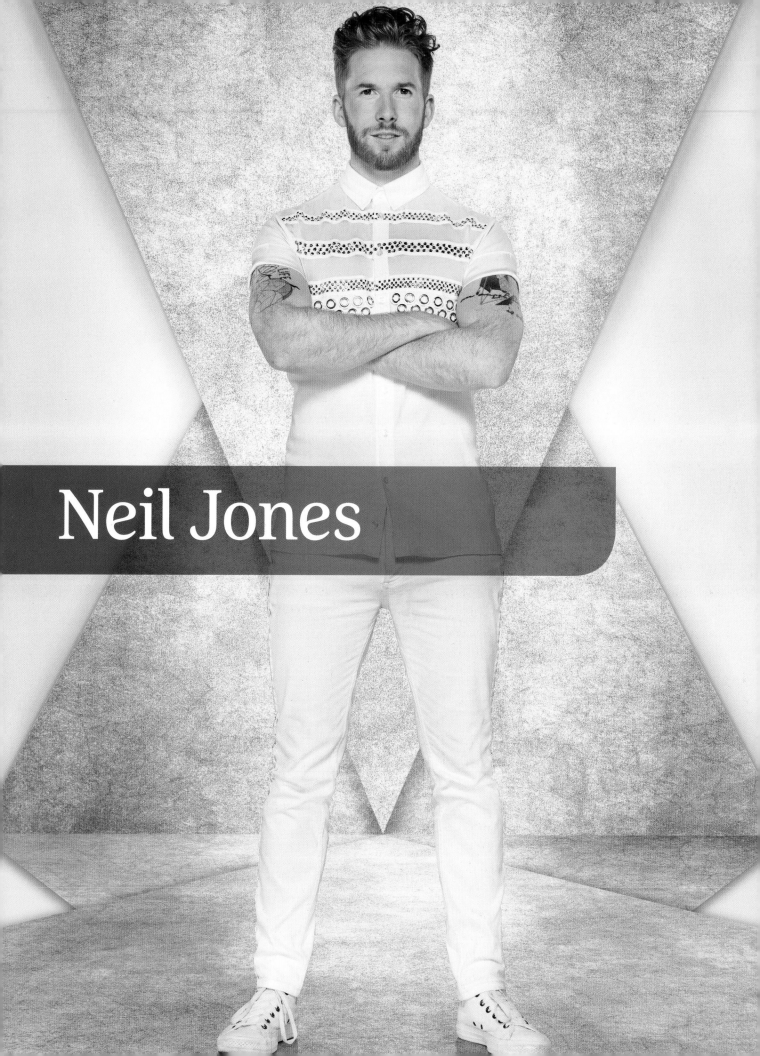

Neil Jones

This year, dancer Neil Jones has his first celebrity partner for the main show, and now that he's paired with Alex Scott, he couldn't be happier.

'I got lucky,' he says. 'The main thing for me was just getting a partner, and I always said, "I don't care who I get, just give me anybody." Then, as we got to know the celebs, I started thinking, "It still doesn't matter, but if I got Alex, that would be great."

So when they announced the partnership I was so elated, I started running and then slid across the room on my knees in a terrible football slide!'

Neil's not the only one in his family who is happy about the pairing.

'My 19-year-old niece is a football player, and before she knew I was getting a partner, she was saying, "I want to come to the show so I can meet Alex once." She was over the moon when she found out I'm actually dancing with her, and she's so excited.'

Born in a British Army Camp in Münster, Germany, Neil took his first ballet classes at the tender age of three before training in tap, modern, ballroom and Latin. He has represented the UK, Finland and the Netherlands and holds 45 dance championship titles – among them, he is the eight-time British National, eight-time Dutch National and four-time World Latin Champion.

In 2008, he met and paired up with fellow *Strictly* pro Katya in Blackpool. Together, they are the undefeated four-time British National Champions and the three-time winners of the World Amateur Latin Championships.

For the last three years, Neil has been a key member of the professional dance team, as well as helping out with choreography. But this year he's going to be saving his best moves for his own routines.

'I'm always full of ideas,' he says. But they don't work with everyone and they might not work with Alex. So I'm trying to get to know her, get to know her favourite music and so on, because I want it all to relate to her.'

Although she's used to training hard, Alex retired from football a year ago and Neil says the first thing he needs to do is get her fit again.

'We will have to start at the beginning but as a sportswoman, she is used to putting in the hours, which will help. She's also used to doing something over and over again without getting bored, and that's important because that's a dancer's life.'

Although he thinks Alex will initially feel more comfortable in Latin, he predicts a flair for ballroom, too.

'She's strong, so I feel that she will be able to get herself into a good frame and keep it. It's just a case of teaching her what a good frame is, so she can nail that.' 'She is a really nice person and a role model for women,' he says. 'All my friends are into football and they think she's great. On top of that, she's so hard working and she really wants to learn.'

Neil has his fingers crossed for a place in the Final, but in the meantime, he says, 'we're just going to try to entertain everyone'.

Meet the *Strictly* Band

The Saturday-night show simply wouldn't be *Strictly Come Dancing* without the amazing live orchestra and singers. Every year, the talented musicians provide the musical backdrop for almost 200 dances, veering from classic Tangos to rock ballads with accomplished ease.

Leading the way is composer and conductor Dave Arch, who abridges the songs into 90-second arrangements before writing parts for the various instruments. On Fridays, the band comes together for the first time to rehearse, ahead of Saturday's crucial live performance.

The core of the orchestra consists of around 13 regular players, with two extra seats to be filled by hired musicians, depending on the instruments needed for that week's show.

'The rhythm section has a drum, a bass, two guitarists, two keyboard players and a percussionist,' explains Dave. 'Then we might have three trumpets, two trombones and three saxophones, but I tweak it if I need to. So there might be one trombone and a French horn, or an accordion instead of a saxophone, depending on the tracks.

'The signature tune and walk-ons have a lot of brass, but some of the pop music doesn't have any brass at all. Whenever I hear a track that has something different, I flag it up with production and we decide what to do about it. If there's a Tango with an accordion and a violin, for instance, I can't do anything big and brassy because I need to lose two brass to do it.'

Occasionally, Dave needs to call upon something more specialist, too. 'We had bagpipes when we played "Flower of Scotland" for Kenny Logan, and for the Argentine Tango we often get a very small South American accordion called a bandoneon.'

The band spends most of Saturday in the pit at the back of the stage and bassist Trevor Barry reveals that, to keep energy levels up, they are constantly passing round Wine Gums and nuts.

1. Hayley Sanderson

Hayley has worked with producers Nile Rodgers and Narada Michael Walden before becoming the house singer at Ronnie Scott's and taking part in various recording sessions – where she met Dave Arch. Before and during live shows, Hayley stretches her vocal cords by blowing bubbles in water through a giant straw!

2. Billy Philips

Billy is a professional singer, guitarist and songwriter from London. This year's Launch Show was his first *Strictly* gig.

3. Andrea Grant

Andrea has toured with the likes of Shirley Bassey, Lisa Stansfield, Robbie Williams and McFly, and joined *Strictly* in series three after getting through open auditions. Before singing, Andrea drinks honey, ginger and hot water.

4. Tommy Blaize

Tommy has worked with legendary artists including Diana Ross, Queen and Amy Winehouse. Tommy protects his vocal cords with a regular intake of pineapple – and always has a jar next to his microphone.

5. Jamie Talbot – Saxophone, Clarinet, Flute and Piccolo

Jamie has played with legends like Ella Fitzgerald, Frank Sinatra and Nelson Riddle, as well as Robbie Williams and Wham!, and was the jazz clarinet soloist at the London 2012 Olympics Opening Ceremony.

His favourite *Strictly* moments include 'watching John Sergeant dragging Kristina Rihanoff across the dance floor as if he was taking the rubbish out'. He also loved playing a hit medley for Gloria Estefan in Blackpool last year. 'She was really impressed by the band!'

6. Phil Todd – Saxophone, Flute and Clarinet

Born and raised in Borehamwood – Phil got his big break when a composer saw him performing with the National Youth Jazz Orchestra (NYJO) and asked him to play on his album. The tracks Phil most loves to play are rock, funk and 'anything contemporary', and he says he loves working with Dave Arch and the band – 'the best musical director and musicians in the country'.

His favourite Strictly memory is 'moving from BBC Shepherd's Bush to Elstree – back to my roots!'

7. Craig Wild – Trumpet

Craig started playing cornet at the age of six and has gone on to perform in many West End shows, and has also worked with music legends including Sir Paul McCartney, Shirley

Bassey and Frank Sinatra Jr.

Craig used to love playing the warm-up song with Bruce Forsyth each week. 'He even came down into the band pit one year when we all wore Brucie masks for a photo with us all!'

8. Simon Gardner – Trumpet

When Simon was 13, his music teacher gave him a trumpet and he was hooked. Although he plays many different styles in course of the show, his favourite is big-band jazz.

'Strictly has music to fit all tastes,' he says. 'and a live band playing live music. That's something I think the public can relate to and appreciate.'

9. Tom Rees-Roberts – Trumpet

Tom has played on every series of Strictly – and features in the original theme tune. Frank Sinatra, Earth, Wind & Fire and Stevie Wonder are among his favourite artists to play on Strictly, and he says he loves the 'spectacular set pieces, like backing Gloria Estefan's Latin medley at Blackpool last year'.

'I love sharing the contestants' dance journey,' he says. 'But my favourite memories are the funny moments, like watching from below when Ann Widdecombe was winched over the band on a wire.'

10. John Parricelli – Guitar

When John moved to London, he began to play jazz gigs and met Trevor Barry, who introduced him to Strictly conductor Dave Arch. John loves playing 'anything with a groove' and says the best thing about Strictly is 'playing with such amazing musicians'.

'Strictly is great because it's live, with all the excitement that brings,' he says. 'And it is something which can bring people together on a Saturday evening.'

11. Alistair White – (Occasional) Trombone

At 16, Lancashire lad Alistair became the youngest ever winner of the Young Jazz Musician of the Year. Since then he has worked with Paul Weller, Kylie Minogue, Aretha Franklin, become the trombonist for Noel Gallagher's High Flying Birds and played in the West End in shows such as The Lion King, Chicago and Dirty Dancing.

12. Andy Wood – Trombone and Tuba

Andy joined the BBC Big Band as the jazz trombone soloist at age 22.

On live shows, we only get one chance and it has to be perfect,' he says. 'But week in, week out, my amazing friends do exactly that. I love how varied the music is – hearing our guitarists Paul and John playing some terrifyingly difficult flamenco stuff live, completely perfectly, then playing 1920s banjo is astonishing.'

13. Paul Clarvis – (Occasional) Percussion

Londoner Paul can be heard on the soundtracks of many films, including Star Wars and the whole Harry Potter series. He was Leonard Bernstein's UK percussionist and helped train the 100 drummers who appeared in the opening of the 2012 London Olympics.

14. Frank Ricotti – Percussion

Proficient on over 20 instruments, Frank says 'It has been my pleasure to play in the Strictly band from series four,' he says. 'It's full of brilliant musicians and is simply the best band on TV.'

15. Trevor Barry – Bass

Eagle-eyed *Strictly* viewers will recognise Trevor from his 'mascot' – his ever-present pork-pie hat.

He has worked with many artists, from Freddie Mercury to Emeli Sandé! Trevor loves playing a wide variety of music and says during a *Strictly* series, 'We play so many songs I can't remember any of them, even as I drive home. Bonkers eh?

'We also look forward to seeing how wardrobe dress up our Dave,' he says. 'It's normally as Dracula or some evil dark lord!'

16. Jeff Leach – Keyboards

Jeff was playing the violin and recorder at six and the cornet and piano by seven.

'I find pleasure in playing nearly all styles,' he says. 'Trying to play the right thing in the right place and the right tone is challenging and a lot of fun.' His favourite *Strictly* memory is playing the *Test Match Special* theme as Graeme Swann flew over his head on a giant cricket bat!

17. Brett Morgan – Drums

Born in London, Brett decided to follow in his drummer dad's footsteps after watching him perform, at the age of six. 'My father Barry inspired me. He was such a great player and mentor for me.

'Playing in the *Strictly* band is not for the faint-hearted,' says Brett. 'But what makes *Strictly* so successful is that we all relate to dancing and trying to improve, and there will always be a piece of music you personally love. *Strictly* brings out the best in people in every way.'

18. Pete Murray – Keyboards

When Pete applied to a music college, he didn't even tell his parents – in case he didn't get in – but success meant a move to London and the start of his musical career.

Pete's favourite thing about *Strictly* is 'listening to my colleagues giving some standout performances. There have been more than a few! It's wonderful to be part of a band of this size, singers included, that always sounds amazing. The fact that the show's live adds a particular buzz as well, and the fact that we're all old friends is an added bonus.'

19. Paul Dunne – Guitar

Paul loves working on *Strictly* and says every year is like a reunion. 'We've all known each other for years, so it's really nice to get together every year. The band is amazing, the professional dancers are incredible, and it's all fun.'

Actor and racing driver Kelvin Fletcher says he is beyond excited to be heading for the dance floor.

'It's been the most surreal week of my life!' he says. 'I'm a massive fan of *Strictly*, so it's incredible. I'm so happy that I can be a part of it. But at the same time, it's bittersweet. I'm coming in on the back of Jamie's injury – I can't imagine going through all this excitement and then having to pull out. He seems like a fantastic guy and I hope he's doing okay.'

The Oldham-born star began attending a local theatre workshop at six, and after leaving school, he appeared in various TV shows, including *Cracker* and *Heartbeat*. In 1996, he landed the role of Andy Sugden in *Emmerdale* and he stayed in the show for two decades. He has now turned his hand to racing and is in the prestigious British GT Championship.

To date, Kelvin's dance experience has been limited to weddings and parties, but he's no stranger to taking off his shirt – his 'signature move' on a night out. And he loves a fake tan.

'I'm a fake-tan addict,' he admits. 'I did *The All New Monty* this year, which was amazing – they gave us all spray tans. I was stood there with Alexander Armstrong, Willie Thorne – all the guys had them. So I'm excited to get tanned again. It's all part of it.

'I can't wait for the costumes, too. When else am I going to get the chance to wear sequins and glitter? No one's ever seen me dress like that. It's a great chance for people to see a different side to me – I'm all for it and will give anything a go.'

The former soap star says he's thrilled to be dancing with Oti, and he's willing to put in the hours to make her proud.

'I pride myself on my work ethic, so if we need to stay in the studio to get a certain dance move right, that's fine,' he says. 'I hope I'll be a good student. I think I'll get frustrated with myself if I can't get a move. I want to get it right. I know it'll feel so good when I do get it. I think I'll really enjoy it.'

Dad-of-two Kelvin says daughter Marnie, three, and one-year-old son Milo will be watching his moves.

'They're only little, but I think they'll love it,' he says. 'I spend most of my time at home dancing with my daughter to things like *Frozen* and I think she'll be really excited to watch me do it for real.'

Although Kelvin says picking up the choreography will be a new experience, he hopes his acting skills will come in handy on the dance floor.

'I'm sure there will be a narrative and a storyline to every performance, so I'd hope I could do that bit right,' he says. 'But the biggest thing for me is the nerves. I am a performer, but this is such new territory and a new skillset. It's live. I don't want to let anyone down and I don't want to let myself down.'

Busy working on his dance steps, Kelvin says he won't be eyeing up the competition. 'I'm competitive when I'm racing, but this is totally different,' he says. 'It's more about not letting myself down and trying to do the best I can. I can't wait to see the others do well, too. I've got an idea of how I'd love to look. I want to be smooth, going around the dance floor like John Travolta. But in reality, that might not be the case.'

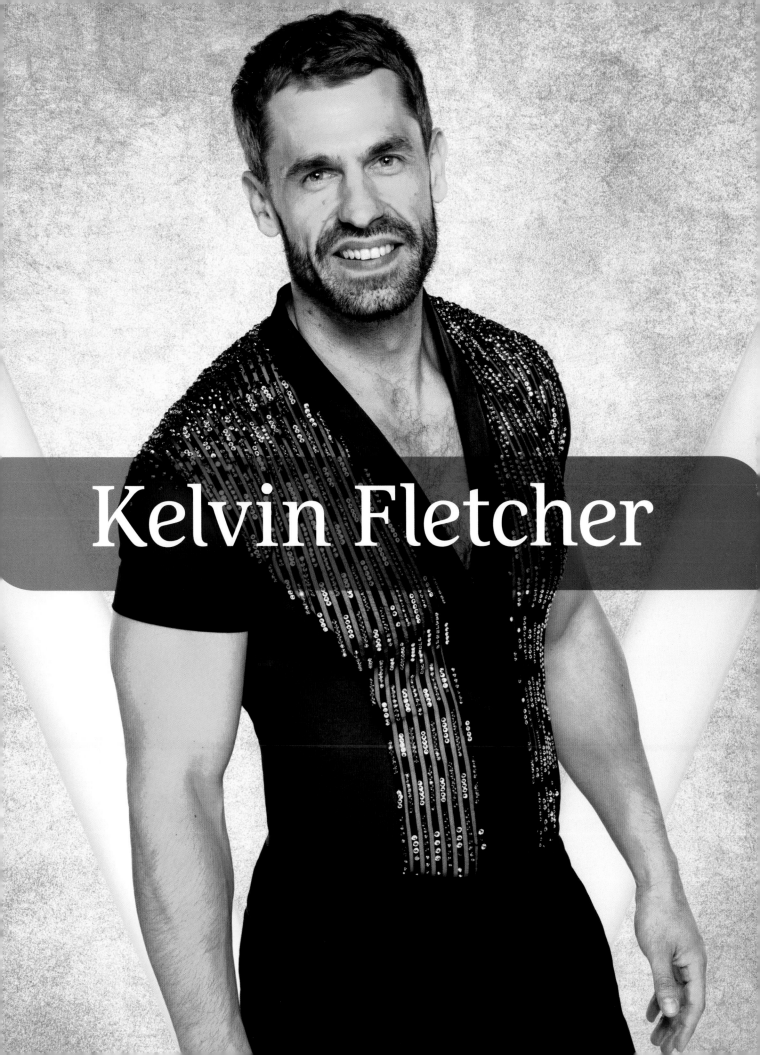

Kelvin Fletcher

Oti Mabuse

South African dancer Oti Mabuse teams up with actor Kelvin Fletcher for series 17, and the pair are already making great progress.

'I'm so grateful to Kelvin for stepping up,' she says. 'It wasn't easy for him to drop all his commitments to be on the show, but he did. I was so happy that his family was able to support him and help him take the opportunity.'

Oti says she was 'devastated' when the news of Jamie's departure from the series came through. 'Jamie and I really hit it off from the get-go,' she says. 'He matched my ambitious mentality and was really hard working. He really wanted to make his mum and nan proud so it hurt a little bit to know that we weren't going to do the series together after all. But I'm glad to be dancing with Kelvin and hope Jamie makes a speedy recovery.'

South African Oti started dancing as a young girl in Pretoria, alongside older sister Motsi – now a *Strictly Come Dancing* judge. After studying civil engineering at university, Oti moved to Germany to pursue her dancing career, soon landing second place in the European Championship Latin in 2014 and first place in German Championship PD Freestyle Latin.

She made her *Strictly* debut with Anthony Ogogo in 2015 and the following year danced her way to the Final with Danny Mac. She partnered the show's first Paralympian, Jonnie Peacock, before hitting a few runs with cricketer Graeme Swann last year.

Although Oti was a teacher to Graeme, she learned a lot from the affable England star. 'Graeme taught me to remember that it's okay to have fun in training, not all work, work, work.'

Oti has already carried her new 'all work and some play' ethos into the training room with Kelvin. 'Kelvin is having so much fun,' she says. 'And he has never danced in his life so he's not super confident, but I love the progress. A late start on the show meant that he missed out on the gentle introduction the other stars had before the Launch Show, but he's been blown away by the incredible response to him.'

Tess Daly

Having been with the show since day one, no one loves the buzz of the *Strictly* Launch Show more than Tess Daly.

'For me, the Launch Show is pivotal because you get to see the celebrities in the *Strictly* environment for the first time, with all the hair and make-up,' she says. 'It's great to see how they react when they first stand on a shiny floor in the studio with an audience, because many of them are out of their comfort zone. But this bunch seems to wholeheartedly embrace the concept. They were like giddy schoolchildren.'

'Alex Scott was a bouncy bundle of energy. She's vivacious, enthusiastic, embracing every aspect of a *Strictly*. Another one to watch is Emma Barton. It was wonderful when Anton was partnered with her, because he was so thrilled – it was the first time ever in *Strictly* history that I've seen him speechless. I'm glad we got that on camera!

'Emma Weymouth is drop-dead gorgeous and certainly looks the part. She's used to running around after two little boys and lots of wild animals at Longleat, so she'll be able to handle anything Aljaž throws at her.

'Karim has a spring in his step and this cool confidence.

'Mike Bushell is hysterical. I have high hopes for his pairing with Katya. I'm expecting lots of laughs.'

Tess thinks Craig may also have met his match in Michelle Visage. 'Fierce and fabulous, Michelle has promised to give Craig as good as she gets. She's a judge on *RuPaul's Drag Race* and she says it like it is. So look out, Craig!'

As well as a fresh line-up, the show has a new judge in Motsi Mabuse, and Tess is excited to welcome her on board.

'Motsi charmed us all early on, she's very empathetic. She's passionate about the celebrities doing their best.'

Last March, after years of telling viewers to 'keep dancing', Tess put her money where her mouth is, as she and Claudia took on the longest ever Danceathon for Comic Relief staying on their feet for 24 hours and raising £1.3 million. 'We did the equivalent of one and a half marathons. Luckily, we had *Strictly* dancers, friends and celebrities dropping in to support us and we raised a ton of cash for a brilliant cause.'

Pros *on* Tour...

For the past decade, the Live Arena Tour has provided fans all over the country with a chance to grab a slice of *Strictly* on their very own doorstep. And this year, a second slice was on offer – as *Strictly Come Dancing: The Professionals* went on tour. Starring ten of the show's amazing dancers – Pasha Kovalev, Dianne Buswell, Giovanni Pernice, AJ Pritchard, Katya Jones, Oti Mabuse, Karen Hauer, Nadiya Bychkova, Neil Jones and Gorka Márquez – the tour allowed dance devotees to get to know the professionals better and, of course, watch some spectacular routines.

'The pro tour is a bit like the arena tour. The audience get to watch some their favourite *Strictly* pro dancers dancing together at the top of the game, so there is a definite dance wow factor! But they are also showing the audience things that they've not seen before, giving a bit more insight into them as people, talking about what it took to get to where they are, so it's biographical too.'

Directed and choreographed by *Strictly*'s creative director Jason Gilkison, the 2019 show was broken down into ten segments (each one presented by a different pro), which cover everything from New York and dance legends Fred Astaire and Gene Kelly,

to memories of competing at Blackpool and *Strictly*'s spectacular show from the Tower Ballroom.

'It was a mini-musical really, and therefore very different to the live arena tour,' says Jason. 'There was storytelling, dancing, and the audience got to know the pros a little bit better. Each of them had something that they delivered, and they were all sewn up together with lots and lots of dancing.'

Although in 2019 The Professionals theatre tour kicked off in May, playing 26 dates around the country in the space of a month, Jason had been working on the concept since November. But the pros had just three

weeks to learn their numbers – which was no mean feat.

'All of them were on the stage almost all of the time,' says Jason. 'When they weren't dancing the lead, they were supporting the other pros. Each one of them did around four or five solos – never with the same partners. Sometimes there were trios, sometimes two couples or all ten of them, so they had a lot to learn in a very short amount of time.

'But all the pros took the show very seriously and by the time rehearsals began, they knew their lines, they knew their choreography, so that made for a lovely rehearsal period and a great creative experience.'

Although it had its own distinctive flavour, the show has the *Strictly* stamp, incorporating the famous neon arches, a live band, led by Gareth Weedon, and live singers Alison Jiear and Patrick Smyth. There was also a whole lot of sparkle on the stage, with a host of amazing outfits designed by Vicky Gill and her team.

'Vicky excelled herself on this tour,' says Jason. 'We were adamant we wanted it to look different from the arena tour that we had earlier in the year, so she came up with fantastic things. Some were traditional outfits that were sparkly, gorgeous, lavish and feathery, but she had added some more contemporary looks, because they were quite a young group, she was able to bend the rules a little.'

With barely a minute offstage for the multiple costume changes, however, some precision timing was necessary to keep the show flowing.

'We're talking ridiculously quick changes,' admits Jason. 'Less than two minutes in some cases, so there was as much choreography backstage as onstage. On the first tech run, no one made the changes [in time], but you keep trying it until eventually those changes work.'

'The pros are really good at knowing how to adapt.

For example, they'd say, "If the buttons were replaced with Velcro, I'd be able to make that change 15 seconds quicker," so they hone in on what's taking the longest and how to make those things move along.'

With 18 different venues in a month, the dancers had little time to settle into their surroundings before launching themselves into the performance, sometimes arriving at the theatre just two hours before curtain-up. 'It was like a touring theatre show, so they have a blueprint which is laid down, so even when they arrived in Blackpool, it was exactly the same set-up as it would have been the night before in Aberdeen,' explains Jason. 'They hit the marks at the same time, a light came on at the same time and it's a slick, well-oiled machine.

As each pro dancer talked, a big screen at the back of the stage plays memorable moments from the TV show. 'It's a trip down memory lane, because the audience can relive the moments they loved on *Strictly Come Dancing*. When we were putting the *Strictly* VT medleys together, we were all in hysterics!'

There were also some familiar favourites among the live routines, including the spine-tingling group dance to "Havana", first performed on the 2018 launch show, and the pros' favourite dances from the past series. As the tour marked the end of Pasha Kovalev's time on *Strictly*, however, it was his *Dirty Dancing* Salsa with Dianne, to the aptly titled "(I've Had) The Time of My Life", which got a standing ovation every night. 'There was a farewell element to Pasha's section, says Fiona, and he got an incredible reaction, which he deserved because he's an incredible dancer. It was very emotional.'

Strictly Come Dancing: The Professionals tour returns in spring 2020.

Despite being a Paralympic gold medallist, ranked number one in his sport, Will Bayley believes his *Strictly* experience could help him up his table tennis game.

'I've never ever danced. I don't expect to be very good on my first week, but that's part of the show,' he says. I'm hoping I'm going to improve. I'm really looking forward to it.

'Hopefully it will also help my sport – I think it will help my balance. I'll be working with amazing, ridiculously talented dancers and I know I can learn a lot from them. I'm hoping to pick up tips from them about keeping fit, balance work and stretching.'

The Kent-born athlete was born with athrogryposis, a congenital condition which leads to an inability to fully extend joints. Remarkably, he also overcame cancer at the age of seven, and it was long spells in hospital that led him to table tennis.

'I was in Great Ormond street hospital having chemo,' he explains. 'My Grandma knew I was always into football and contact sports like rugby, but because I couldn't do that in a hospital bed she bought me a mini table tennis table. I'd play that against my mum and any family who came in to visit me – and found I was quite good at it. When I left hospital I joined a club and continued playing, buying a table for my garage. I played every day from there.'

Will went on to represent Kent in the men's team at 17, before winning a silver medal at the 2012 Paralympics in London and a gold in Rio four years later. He has been ranked world number one since 2012 and was awarded an MBE in 2017.

Although his disability affects all four limbs Will – who is partnered with Janette Manrara – is determined to make his mark on the dance floor in order to inspire kids who have similar conditions.

'My condition affects the muscles in all four limbs,' he says. 'It's really difficult to build muscle and keep muscle. It affects my hands and my feet, so dancing is going to be really challenging.

'When I was growing up I didn't see anyone on TV who had the same disability as me. Until I joined the Paralympic team the only person I knew who was similar to me was my mum.

'I remember meeting Lee Pearson, a champion dressage rider who also has arthrogryposis. It was the first time I can remember that I wasn't embarrassed or ashamed of my disability. He won loads of gold medals and I was telling anyone who'd listen that I had the same disability as him. I felt proud.

'So I need to do it. I want kids with the same or similar conditions to be able to look up to someone and see them dancing. I would have liked that when I was a kid.'

Will's lightning reflexes around the table tennis table could prove handy in the Quickstep and Jive and he admits he prefers to be fast on his feet.

'I'm limited in my knowledge of the dances but I quite enjoy the faster dances because they suit my personality,' he says. 'I think it will be harder to get my personality across with something like the Waltz. But we'll see how it goes.'

One thing he is looking forward to is getting dressed up in custom-made outfits – especially his dancing shoes.

'I struggle finding shoes because of the shape of my feet,' he explains. 'But I've spoken to the costume team and they're going to help me. Maybe finally they will be able to find me some shoes that actually fit me!'

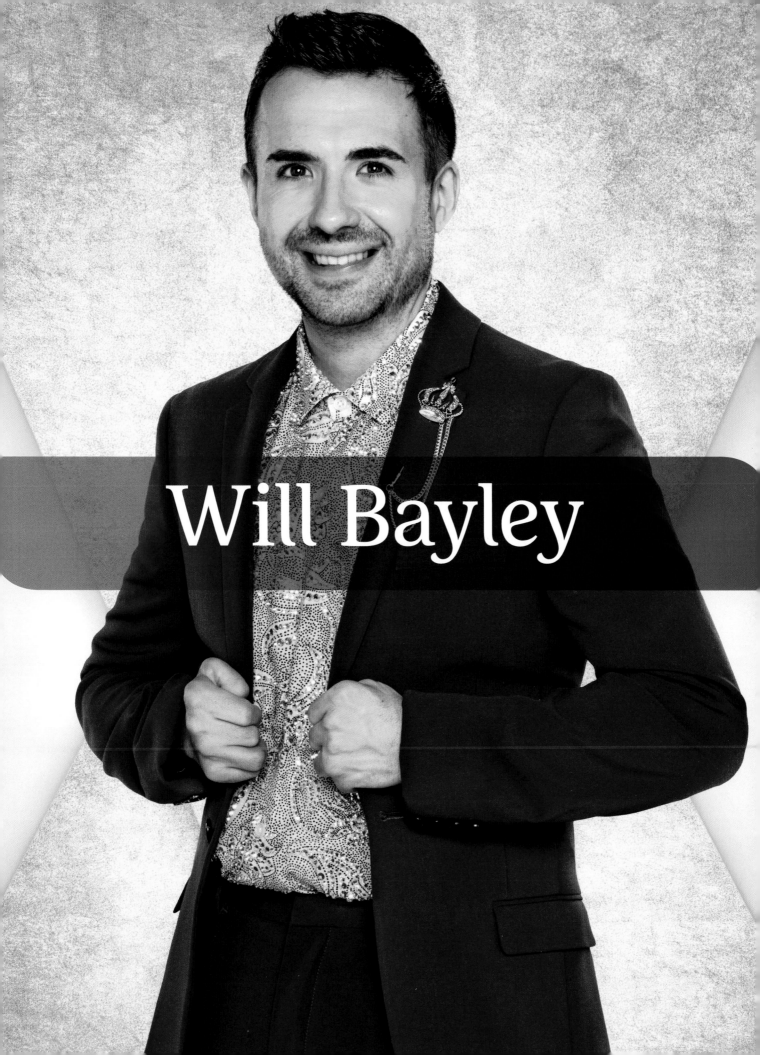

Will Bayley

Janette Manrara

Pocket-rocket Janette Manrara is very excited after landing Paralympic table-tennis champ Will Bayley as her series-17 celebrity.

'I'd met Will a few times before *Strictly* and I think his whole story and everything he represents is incredible,' she says. 'He's so determined, so enthusiastic and such a positive guy. He really wants to inspire people to do what they want to do and follow their dreams without letting anything holding them back.'

Although Will has athrogryposis, which affects his hands and feet, Janette says he has a few secret weapons up his sleeve, which she plans to make the most of.

'Because he's an athlete, he has a very strong mind and he's very determined. In his head, nothing is impossible. But his strength is also in his enthusiasm – he loves pushing himself. When we did the first group number, he had an incredible energy in his face, and he brought the room to life. He's just incredible to watch.'

Janette was born in Miami and came late to dance, learning in her spare time while studying for a degree at Florida International University. Trained in ballroom, ballet, pointe, jazz, hip-hop and Salsa, she and now-husband Aljaž joined *Strictly* in 2013. In previous years, she has danced with Peter Andre, Aston Merrygold, Julien Macdonald and Melvin Odoom, and in 2014 she made it to the Semi-finals with Jake Wood. Last year, she danced with Dr Ranj Singh and they were the sixth couple to leave the show.

'Ranj has become one of my best friends and we still talk almost every day,' she says. 'Like Will, he was determined. He was still doing very long shifts at the hospital, sometimes up to 36 hours straight, but no matter how tired he was, no matter how much he had going on, he wanted to rehearse and do a good job.'

With her new partner, Janette is 'thinking outside the box' to tailor her choreography around his condition.

'Will has no use of his wrists or ankles and he can't really use his hands or feet properly,' she says. 'He can use his knees, his elbows and the rest of his body, but his feet are contracted, so he's got a tiny base to balance on.'

'While he's playing table tennis, he's quick on his feet, and that's an advantage. It's going be interesting to choreograph and create, so I'm looking forward to that challenge.'

Although the pair initially missed a week of training, as Will was competing in tournaments, Janette says they can more than make up for lost time.

'After the championship, I have him all day every day, which is great,' she says, 'and I know he's going to want to put in the hours and make whatever he does amazing.'

Which Dance are You?

Are you a hot-blooded party lover, with that Latin vibe?

Or a cool ballroom queen, elegant and organised?

Follow our fun flowchart to find out which dance suits you.

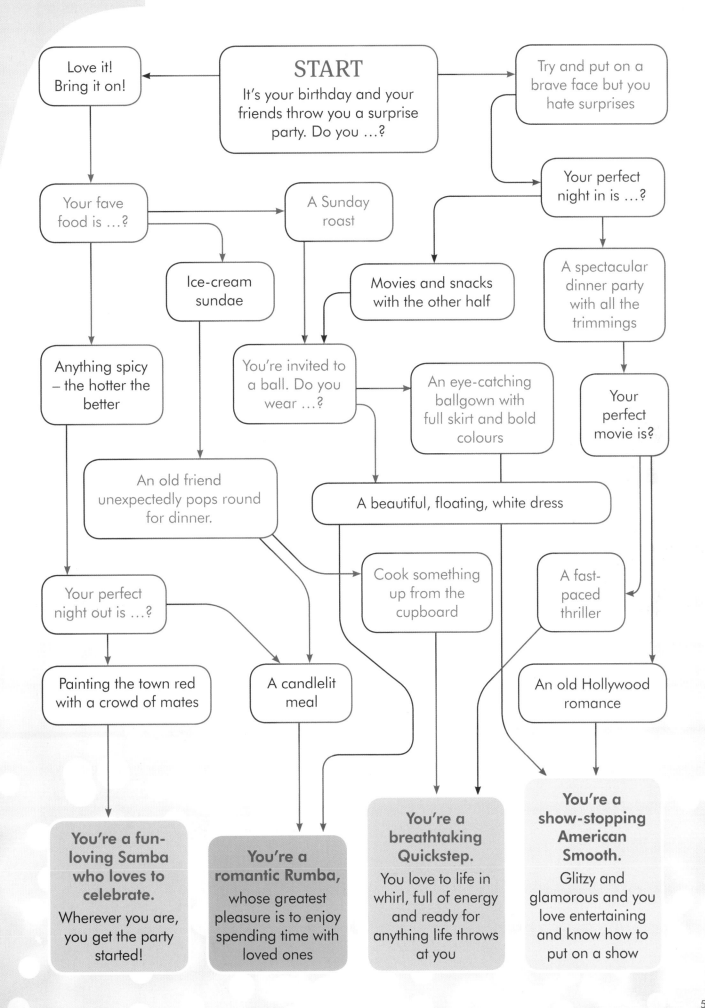

START
It's your birthday and your friends throw you a surprise party. Do you …?

Love it! Bring it on!

Try and put on a brave face but you hate surprises

Your fave food is …?

A Sunday roast

Your perfect night in is …?

Ice-cream sundae

Movies and snacks with the other half

A spectacular dinner party with all the trimmings

Anything spicy – the hotter the better

You're invited to a ball. Do you wear …?

An eye-catching ballgown with full skirt and bold colours

Your perfect movie is?

An old friend unexpectedly pops round for dinner.

A beautiful, floating, white dress

Your perfect night out is …?

Cook something up from the cupboard

A fast-paced thriller

Painting the town red with a crowd of mates

A candlelit meal

An old Hollywood romance

You're a fun-loving Samba who loves to celebrate.

Wherever you are, you get the party started!

You're a romantic Rumba, whose greatest pleasure is to enjoy spending time with loved ones

You're a breathtaking Quickstep. You love to life in whirl, full of energy and ready for anything life throws at you

You're a show-stopping American Smooth. Glitzy and glamorous and you love entertaining and know how to put on a show

Bruno Tonioli

After an incredible Final last year, Bruno is looking forward to being back in his judge's chair to find out what the class of 2019 has to offer. And the Italian judge has a word of advice for the new line-up.

'Remember, it's not only about the dancing,' he says. 'Last year, the Final was very, very good because they all came up with great ideas and that's what they have to do this year.'

Once the celebrities get to the Final, says Bruno, it's all about wooing the audiences at home. 'The judges' votes are just for guidance at that stage, so you really have to capture the imagination of the public to win.'

What do you think of the 2019 line-up?

Once again, it's a good mixture. I'm excited to see Michelle Visage because I love *Ru Paul's Drag Race*, and as a personality she's great. Anneka Rice is a lovely lady, warm and friendly, so I'm looking forward to seeing her.

Who have you got your eye on?

Alex Scott could be one to watch. She looks very capable, and all those who come from the world of sport are great competitors.

Catherine Tyldesley looks like she would have good poise.

Saffron Barker is an influencer, so she's following in the footsteps of Joe Sugg – and look how well he did. And this year we have a Lady, Emma Weymouth. It will be fun to see how she does.

Do you think there will be some surprises in the pack?

We can't tell who is going to have talent on the dance floor until we've seen the first two dances. They need two rounds to find their footing. So with *Strictly* there are always surprises. Look at Stacey Dooley and Joe Sugg, last year. Things happen that you would never expect, and that's what's good about it.

How do you think Motsi Mabuse will do as the new judge?

She'll be excellent. I'm excited because she's very experienced as a dancer and she's judged the show in Germany for years, so she knows what the gig is. She's a beautiful lady and I'm all for it. I think she will bring a lot of spark and excitement to the panel.

TV diva **Michelle** Visage is planning to bring some drama to the dance floor after a milestone birthday persuaded her to take on a new challenge.

'I turned 50 last September and I have done many things in my life, but I have never ballroom danced,' she says. 'Ballroom is something I have been obsessed with for years but have never taken a lesson. The tans, the hips, the fringe, the faces, the drama – my God, I love it all.

'I am so excited to try something that I have always admired and so thrilled to be a 'woman of a certain age' who isn't afraid to work hard and get on that dance floor and shake what I've got. I cannot believe I'm doing *Strictly*!'

Born in New Jersey, Michelle trained at the American Musical and Dramatic Academy in New York for two years before becoming a singer, joining girl group Seduction in 1989. From her late teens she was active in the New York club scene, where she was nicknamed 'Cara', meaning 'face' in Spanish which inspire her to change her surname from Schupack to the French word, 'Visage'. She went on to become a radio presenter, sharing many broadcasts with her friend RuPaul, before becoming a judge on the hit show *RuPaul's Drag Race*.

Now going from judge to contestant, Michelle thinks her experience will help her take criticism on the chin.

'I wouldn't do it for any other show, but *Strictly* is something I have been wanting to do for quite some time,' she says. 'I will take my critiques and use them because I know what it's like to sit on the other side of the judges' panel.

The flamboyant Drag Race judge is used to dramatic dresses and sparkles so the wardrobe team can have a field day, as far as she's concerned. 'The one part of doing *Strictly* that I am actually used to are the costumes,' she admits. 'I wear the hair, the lashes, the sequins and glitter on a daily basis – I am a female drag queen after all – so this is the one area where I will be in my comfort zone!' Despite her musical background, Michelle says she has no dance training other than a few ballet and tap lessons at the age of seven. 'I am a singer so I have rhythm, which definitely helps, but a dancer I am definitely not… yet.'

For the duration of the show, Michelle has left husband David and daughters, Lillie and Lola at home in California but she's hoping to see them in the audience.

'My youngest daughter's really excited,' she says. 'Hopefully she'll get over here towards the end because no matter what, all the celebs do a dance for the final. My husband will come over then too but my other daughter is at university, so she's living her own life.'

Michelle is hoping taking part in *Strictly* will inspire her daughters and other women.

'I'm in this for myself, for my daughters, I want to do this to be a positive role model, to say: 'You can do anything at any age.' Nothing should stop you ever and that's what I want to do.'

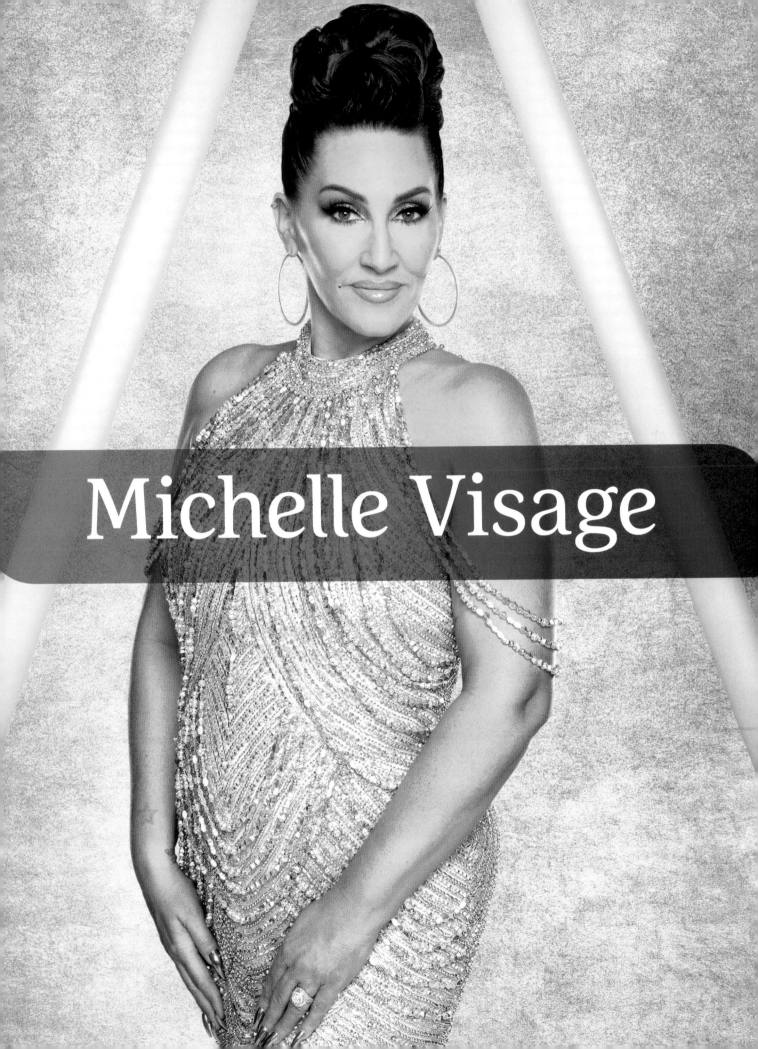

Michelle Visage

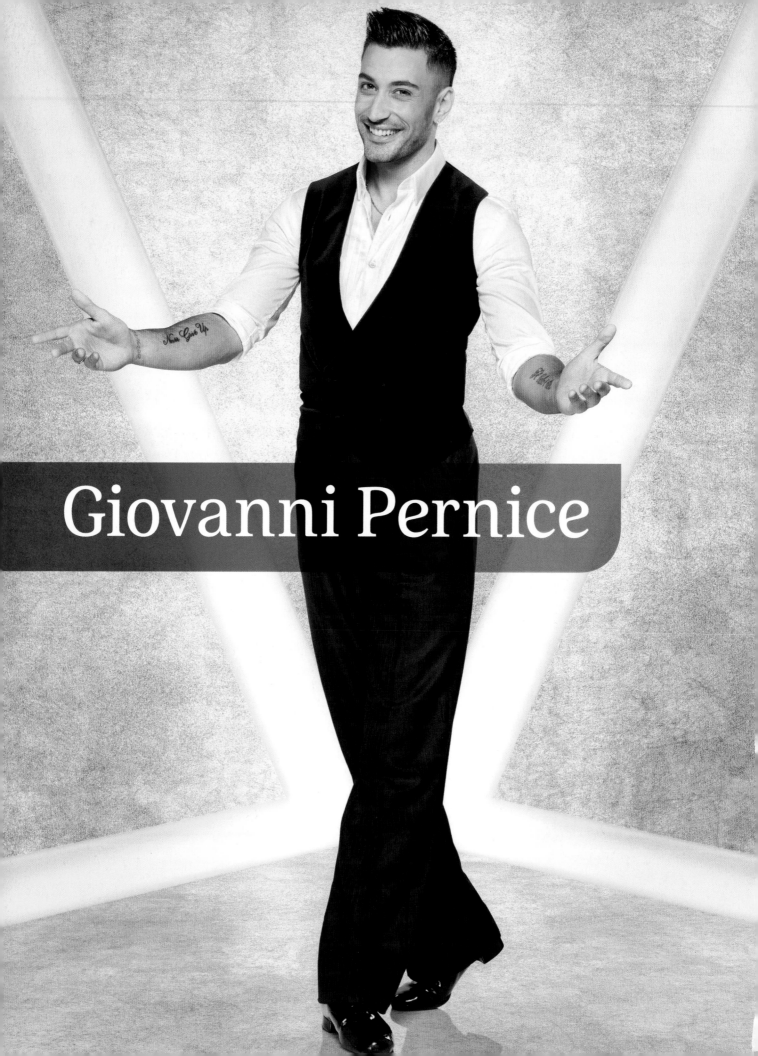

Giovanni Pernice

Three-time finalist Giovanni Pernice has plenty of ideas for dance partner Michelle Visage.

'I'm really happy and excited to be sharing the experience with Michelle,' says Giovanni.

She's funny and sassy and I'm looking forward to creating something for her around her personality. We have got some dramatic routines lined up, but first I need to teach her good technique.

Although Michelle has had little dance experience, Giovanni says she is looking to put the hours in.

'She is a hard worker,' he says. Nothing will come naturally if you haven't done much dancing before. But she's a very elegant lady, so I think ballroom will be no problem at all.'

Born in Sicily, Giovanni took up dance at a young age, and at 14, he moved to Bologna to study dance under some of the best teachers in the world. In 2012 he won the Italian Championships.

In his first *Strictly* series in 2015, he danced his way to the Final with Georgia May Foote, and he has repeated the feat twice since, with Debbie McGee and, last year, with Faye Tozer.

'Last year, I was very impressed with my work,' he laughs. 'In fact, our Couple's Choice Theatre/Jazz and our week-three Quickstep were great, our showdance was good – if you ask me, they're all amazing! 'I loved the puppet dance to "The Lonely Goatherd" because that was different, something that you haven't seen before on *Strictly*. And I was pleased that Faye wanted to do it, because she was one of the celebs who was up for trying anything and she looked amazing.'

With each celebrity, Giovanni takes a different approach in training, and he never knows what to expect at the beginning of the run.

'Every time, it's like opening a new Christmas present,' he says. 'You never know what will happen. Every year is different, so the key is to treat everybody differently. You have to be able to understand the communication between you and your partner, because if you share a good connection with them, then everything gets easier. I've never had a partner like Michelle, she's very, very, sassy!' I can't wait to see what we achieve.

Couple's Choice Dances

As every *Strictly* contestant knows, ballroom and Latin dances aren't just about the footwork; they come with a strict set of rules that must be followed. But, as of last year they get to rip up the rulebook and throw caution to the wind with the Couple's Choice dance.

The first new dance to be introduced into the competition since the Charleston in 2009, the Couple's Choice allowed the pro and celeb to choose from three styles – Street/Commercial, Contemporary and Theatre/Jazz. In series 16, Lauren Steadman and AJ Pritchard were the first to take up the challenge, scoring 24 for their Contemporary dance while Faye Tozer and Giovanni Pernice took their Jazz number to the Final, scoring a perfect 40 in the process.

For head choreographer Jason Gilkison, the new dances are a welcome addition to the series, which began in 2004 with just eight couples and nine dances.

'For a long time we've been looking for a dance style to add because the series is now longer,' he explains. 'But we wanted something that could be bespoke for each celebrity, and give their personality a chance to come out.'

With no technical limitations and no rules, Jason says the judges are looking for completely different pointers in the Couple's Choice dances.

'We don't want the couples to play safe,' says Jason. 'If they do a Rumba, there are rules they have to follow. In Jazz, Contemporary and Street they can do lifts, floorwork and whatever they want. It's really important that, given that opportunity, they push it as far as they can go.'

With no formal steps to worry about, the celebrity needs to throw themselves into the storytelling if they want to impress the likes of Craig and Bruno.

'The judges, in these three styles in

particular, want to see the couples really disappear into those genres,' explains Jason. 'Whereas the other dances on the show are very technical – so they're looking for heels and toes, etc. – these must be character driven. The judges will be looking beyond the footwork and looking for them to really encompass the character. It's like a minishowdance. We want each celebrity to be able to have a moment where they can really shine as much as possible.'

So what are the judges looking for in each dance?

Theatre/Jazz
Think showbiz pizzazz and all that jazz! The judges will want to see a routine that belongs in a West End musical or a Hollywood movie, using soft shoe, tap or even burlesque.

'Musical theatre is something Craig has been immersed in all his life, so this is his world,' says Jason. 'He and the other judges are looking for the couple to take us onto that stage, to transport us to that world.'

Street/Commercial
Taking its cue from modern music videos, this dance needs to be urban, incorporating styles such as hip-hop, breakdancing and funk.

'This speaks to Bruno's background as a dancer and choreographer,' says Jason. 'The judges will want it to be down and dirty. We want that street value and urban grit.'

Contemporary
A fluid and lyrical style of dance, using elements of ballet and modern dance. 'The judges want it to affect us emotionally,' says Jason. 'The celebrity might be revisiting an emotion they've had in their life, putting their own experiences into the dance with a beautiful song that moves them. It's about making sure you really absorb yourself in that music and that character.'

As *Strictly*'s first aristocrat, Viscountess Emma Weymouth, has attended her fair share of society balls, but she admits ballroom is not her forte.

'I love dancing, but I'm not a trained dancer,' she says. 'And I wish I could dance properly, so to be trained by an incredible professional is a dream come true. I'm really grateful. We all watch the show on TV, and so far it has been as incredible as I imagined. I haven't stopped smiling and laughing.'

As the mother of two small boys – John, four, and Henry, two – Emma says she has 'no dancing style' to speak of but loves Bruno Mars and Stevie Wonder.

'I just dance with my friends and my children, so at the moment my dancing is very casual,' she says. 'It's just fun. So I am a completely blank canvas and can't wait for Aljaž to teach me. Which is why I said yes to *Strictly* in a heartbeat.'

London-born Emma has a successful modeling career, working with Dolce & Gabbana, Fiorucci and Harrods. In June 2013, she wed Ceawlin Thynn, Viscount Weymouth, the son of the Marquess of Bath. She now helps to run the stately home and Safari park at Longleat, in Wiltshire.

To minimize time away from her children, Emma is hoping to do most of her training close to home – and possibly in one of the many rooms at Longleat House. 'I'll have somewhere to rehearse in London, but because of my two children, I want to be able to go home and do it there,' she says. 'There are some big rooms, but I'm not sure the floor is right. We'll have to see.

'The schedule is always quite full, but this is my full-time job now for hopefully quite a few months. 'This job transcends normal working hours. I want to train as much as I physically can. It's part of the discipline, part of the challenge and part of the experience.

Everyone who has done it says it is very intense, but it is such an honour to be doing it.'

Although the dancing will be a challenge, Emma says one of the hardest things was keeping the show a secret. 'I was so nervous to tell anyone,' she says. 'I didn't tell anyone but my husband, because we weren't allowed to for a very long time. I couldn't tell my own mum. When we were finally allowed to I said, "Sit down. I have some news." And they all cried! Everyone's been so thrilled, and I've never received so many messages.'

As a fashionista, Emma is looking forward to putting on the sparkle. 'I love the outfits,' she says. 'I love that the dresses are not only beautifully made, but they are built for physical exertion. So they're heavy but constructed immaculately, handbeaded, such beautiful things. Also they have to be extra sparkly to look good under the lights. There is a lot to consider and the team is so talented. I can't wait to go on the journey, to see how all the bits of the jigsaw fit together: the hair, the make-up, the styling, the music and the dancing. I hope I can do it justice.'

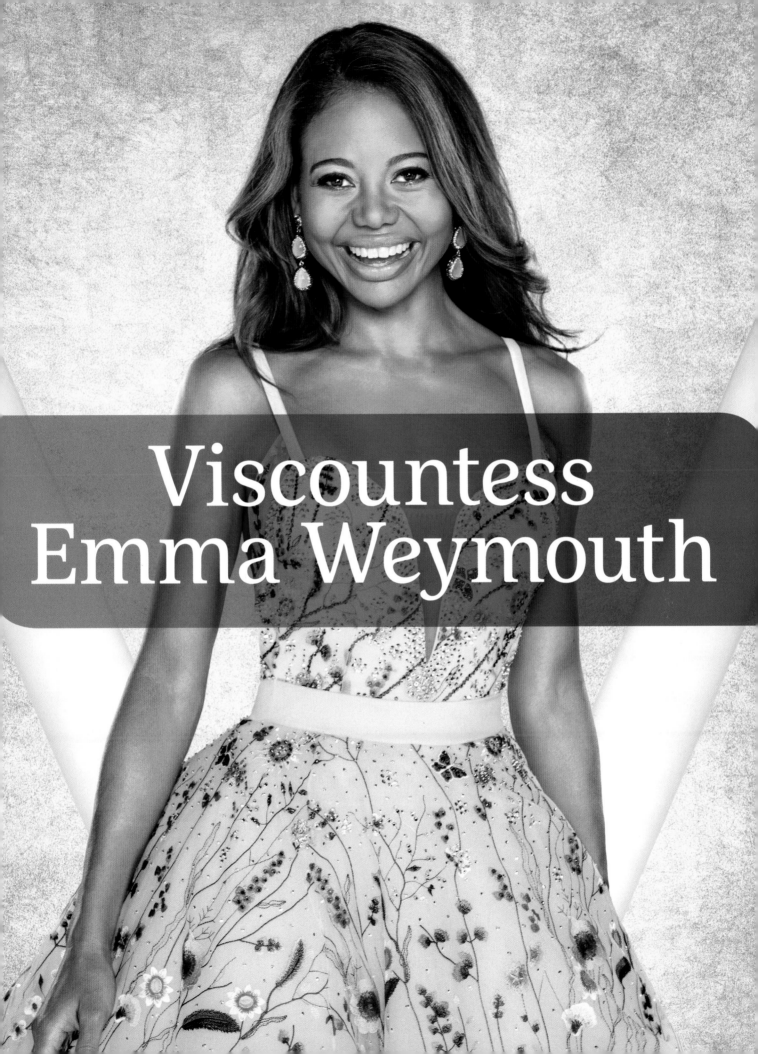

Viscountess
Emma Weymouth

Aljaž Škorjanec

Former *Strictly* champ Aljaž is delighted with his new dance partner, Emma Weymouth – and not just because they are getting on famously. The Slovenian dancer is hoping he will get up close and personal with the lions, giraffes and monkeys at the family's safari park at Longleat.

'I'm really excited,' he admits. 'I love animals and I can't wait to see the safari park. They have all sorts of animals, including lions, tigers and red pandas, which are cute. So I'm chuffed to bits that I'm going to go there.'

Although Emma is his third model, including winner Abbey Clancy, she is *Strictly*'s first aristocrat. 'She is so down to earth, people are just going to think she is lovely. People are just going to think she is lovely.'

Growing up in a small town in Slovenia, Aljaž signed himself up for dance classes, at the age of five, without telling his parents. He went on to be the 19-time Slovenian National Champion in ballroom, Latin and Ten Dance. In his first year of *Strictly*, in 2013, he made his mark by lifting the trophy with Abbey, and four years later he made the Final again, with Gemma Atkinson. Last year he got to week nine with newsreader Kate Silverton.

'I was really happy with how the series went and I was really proud of all of our dances,' he says. 'Kate fell in love with dancing and I was proud we got to Blackpool, because she deserved to get there.'

Starting from scratch again this year, he says Emma has no dance experience, but he sees a 'natural talent' in her. 'She's a beautiful blank canvas for me and we get along really well' he says. 'If you get along with someone, it's easy to be a teacher and easy to be a student, so it's going to be a joy.' As a teacher, Aljaž says he can use Emma's experience of fashion shows to his advantage.

'The last time I danced with a model was with Daisy Lowe, and she was brilliant, as was Abbey,' he says. 'Doing a dance and walking down the runway are two very different things, but if I can tap into that self-belief and confidence, I can translate that onto a dance floor. I'll tell her to imagine it is a runway, there are four judges that are just fashion critics. Hopefully that will help.'

Aljaž also thinks that, with a model's height and poise, Emma will take easily to the posture of the ballroom hold.

'I can't wait to get into a ballroom frame,' he says. 'Everyone knows how much I love it. If I could, I would live in the ballroom frame! I think it's going to suit her. Plus, I think she's also going to have a flavour for the Latin dances.'

As always, Aljaž is looking forward to the group dances and says kicking off the series by dancing with Kylie Minogue has already gone down as a highlight. 'It was so cool,' he says. 'The Launch Show is so important to us pros and to everyone who loves the show, and to have Kylie onstage with us made it even more special. So we were all really excited – and I'm proud of it!'

Claudia Winkleman

As always, Claudia Winkleman was over the moon to be reunited with the *Strictly* family at this year's red carpet event – with the added bonus of Kylie Minogue.

'The red carpet launch was honestly more exciting than my wedding!' she jokes. 'It was amazing to have Kylie there. She was so enthusiastic, I loved her medley so we all felt incredibly lucky. Every year, I forget about the magic of dancing, mainly because I've got a rubbish memory, but then I see the pros dancing on stage with the lights and an amazing crowd, and I'm under the spell again.'

Although it's early days for the contestants, Claudia felt they were all showing promise and she was impressed by how quickly they bonded. 'There already feels like such camaraderie,' she says. 'They're looking after each other, having a laugh and it feels fantastic. They run as a pack.'

Claudia is looking forward to seeing what each one of them can achieve on the dance floor.

'I'm slightly obsessed with Emma Weymouth,' she laughs. 'I'm hoping she's going to invite us all down to Longleat for a sleepover. Catherine is so sweet, bubbling over with excitement. Chris is hilarious and Karim is brilliant. I could go on. I love them all.'

Now in her sixth year of presenting the live shows, Claudia is always on hand to calm any nerves in the early weeks.

'I think the period before they've been paired up is hard for them because they must feel a bit lost, even though they have each other,' she says. 'But once they've got a partner that's it. Our pros are the best in the world and will make them feel great and bring out the best in them.

'At the beginning of the series they are very nervous and I feel it's my job to look after them in my little area.'

Getting along with the cast does have its downside for the presenters – as someone has to be eliminated every week. 'It's horrible when they leave,' says Claudia. 'The first time somebody has to leave the competition, everyone is devastated. It's almost like we'd forgotten that bit. We are all so excited about what they are wearing and what dance they are doing and then they're awaiting their fate under the spotlights and you always think 'Why can't everyone stay?''

Claudia is looking forward to seeing Motsi Mabuse in full judge mode. 'She's adorable, warm, kind and funny, she's an amazing dancer herself too.'

The former It Takes Two presenter is happy to see Rylan Clark-Neal joining Zoe Ball on the weekday show. 'The Rylan and Zoe pairing made me do an actual star jump,' she says. 'I love It Takes Two, I love Zoe and

I never miss one so I think it's a brilliant idea.' While Claudia has never broken in her dancing shoes as a Strictly contestant, she and co-presenter Tess completed a 24-hour Danceathon for Comic Relief in March – raising over £1million. Afterwards an exhausted Claudia revealed, 'I never want to dance again . . . I don't like movement.'

It seems months of recovery haven't changed her mind. Asked which Strictly dance summed up her own personality, Claudia is clear. 'If there was lying down and napping dance, that would be the one for me.'

In his work as a children's presenter Karim Zeroual is used to dressing up and once wore a hot dog costume. So he can't wait to be let loose in *Strictly*'s famous wardrobe department.

'I'm embracing the Lycra and sequins a hundred per cent,' he says. I want wide flares, Cuban heels to give me a couple of inches on my height, and wild hairstyles. I love all that. It's a strong 50 per cent of the *Strictly* experience for me. Put that together with the chance to dance and you've got a real fun few months.'

London – born Karim attended Sylvia Young Stage School and launched his career as a child actor in the West End, starring in *Chitty Chitty Bang Bang*, *The Far Pavilions* and *The Lion King*. Between 2011 and 2015, he starred as Sadiq in sci-fi drama *The Sparticle Mystery*, which had over two million hits on BBC iPlayer. He has been a regular presenter on CBBC since 2014.

Although he had dance lessons at drama school and starred in West End musicals, Karim says his previous experience could prove more of a hindrance than a help.

'At drama school I was training to be an actor but I did dabble in ballet,' he says. 'I love street dance, which helps me with musicality and picking up choreography, but with a lot of the styles in ballroom and Latin it is quite hard to get out of the street style. I have a tendency to urban everything and make everything street dance so that doesn't help my posture or ballroom hold.'

Karim has grown up watching the show with his mum, who is over the moon to see him take part.

'I've always been a fan of the show,' he says. 'Sometimes I'd be out with my friends on Saturday nights and I'd come home and my mum had her favourite dances recorded. She'd get me to watch them with her.

'When we had to keep the secret, I was quite good and I only told my mum. But within one hour my mum had told her friend Debbie. Mum! I told you not to tell anyone!'

Partnered with Amy Dowden, the presenter is hoping her teaching style is 'friendly and fun – but firm.'

'I'm quite energetic, so I need someone to reel me in sometimes,' he says. 'I am here to work hard. Hopefully Amy and I will have a good balance.'

While he wants to throw himself into every dance, he's a little nervous about throwing his dance partner around.

'I am worried about any lifts as I'm quite small,' he says. 'The serious dances will also be challenging. Any dance where I have to be serious and lead the lady... I don't consider myself to be much of a leading man so I think I might struggle with that.'

But the main aim for Karim is to learn a new skill and enjoy the experience.

'I've had friends on *Strictly* before who have said how amazing the journey is,' he says. 'I love music and I love performing, and I have since I was a young kid. Now I'm learning a new skill and having a chance to perform on the BBC which is really incredible. I just want to do the best I can, enjoy myself, have fun and make friends.'

Karim Zeroual

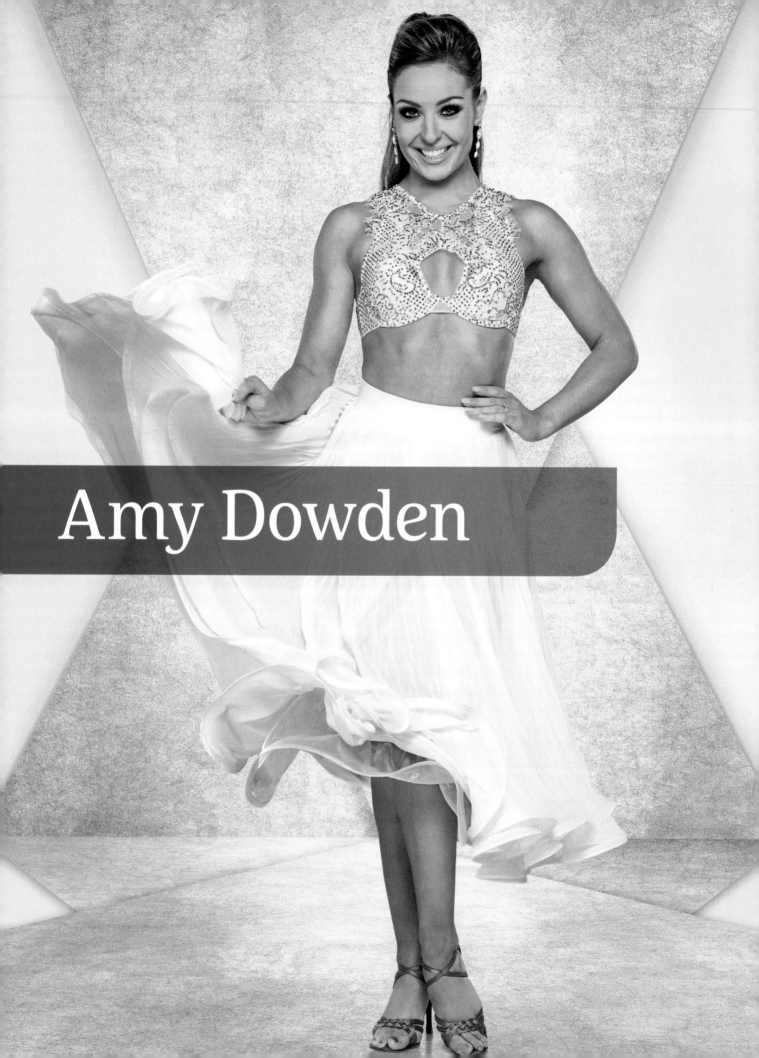

Amy Dowden

Welsh wonder Amy Dowden is dancing with CBBC presenter Karim Zeroual and has already spotted some potential.

'As a dancer, you just know when somebody's got some musicality and a little bit of star quality, and he definitely has that,' she says. 'Now it's up to me to bring it out of him!'

While Karim has a little bit of dance experience, having performed in West End musicals as a child, Amy says his current style is hip-hop and street dance, which could actually prove a disadvantage.

'Street is about as far as you can possibly get from ballroom,' she says. 'A lot of the techniques you use in street, I'm going to be asking him to forget. In some respects, it helps that he is used to picking up routines, but in other ways it will go against him. In terms of posture, in terms of range, your feet and isolation of the body movements, it won't help him. Sometimes it's better to start with a blank canvas.'

While it might help Karim in the Couple's Choice round, Amy says her new dance partner is happy to wipe the slate clean.

'He wants to embrace the whole ballroom and Latin style and he wants to learn,' she says. 'He's quite keen and he'll be pushing himself out of his comfort zones.'

Born in Caerphilly, Amy has been dancing since she was eight and remains one of the highest-ranking ballroom and Latin professionals in the UK. A four-time National Championship Finalist, she became the British National Champion in 2017 with dance partner and now fiancé Ben Jones. She joined *Strictly* the same year, partnering Brian Conley and leaving in week five, and last year she and partner Danny John-Jules made it to week ten.

'Danny was a very quick learner, very talented, and he produced some great numbers,' she says. 'We had some magical moments on *Strictly* together and we managed to get the first 10 of the series, my first ever 10, for our Jive. That's the dance I will remember always.'

This year, Amy is having her third shot at getting into the Final and is preparing to work Karim hard. But she insists there will be plenty of fun along the way.

'Karim said he wants someone to be firm with him and that's definitely me because I'm a perfectionist,' she says. 'He also says he has too much energy, but that's fine too – I can find ways to use that energy up, don't you worry!

'Everyone's journey is different. My aim is for him to have the most amount of fun, to learn as much as he can and to have the best time on this journey. I want him to love every moment of it, to take it week by week and to be judging his own journey, not comparing it to anyone else's.'

The couple have already hit it off in the rehearsal room. 'I already know we're going to get on so well,' says Amy. 'The first day we spent together was so much fun. We're quite similar ages, we're into the same music and things, and conversation is so easy. I can't wait to work with him.'

While aiming for the Final, Amy admits there's another big benchmark she really wants to hit.

'I've not made it to Blackpool yet, so I would love to do that,' she says. 'And I'd obviously love to make it all the way, but so would everybody. We're all very competitive. But we'll take it week by week and I'll do all I can.'

Lights, Camera, Action

From the dining hall at Hogwarts to a dusty prairie in the Wild West, the *Strictly* studio can be instantly transformed into a magical world with endless possibilities. Dancers can twirl against a backdrop of falling snow or play out a dramatic Paso Doble amid a raging fire. And while props play a huge part in the 90-second makeover, lighting and graphics complete the illusion, using a high-tech lighting rig, floor projections and high-resolution video screens.

Four screens in the arch provide the backdrop, while screens on the balconies and behind the audience add the panoramic view, and projectors transform the floor into anything from a chess board to a raging sea.

The video screens are fed by huge computers, 5 feet tall and 3 feet square, which are hidden behind arches at the back of the studio and linked to a computer desk in the lighting gallery, beside the main stage. For the floor projection, the computer splits the image into sections and feeds it to six projectors, which hang from the ceiling. So, while it may look like one image, the effect is actually six merged into one.

Around 900 colour-changing lights, from the LED strips on the arch to spots on the ceiling, add to the ambience.

Graphics designer David Newton and lighting director David Bishop begin planning the professional group dances in June, but for the couples' dances, they have just over a week to work with the other production departments to create the right concept.

'It used to be that we would get the name of the track on rehearsal day or the night before and we would come up with ideas, but now we have all the graphics and screens, it's all tied in to a much larger creative,' says David Newton. 'We can place each dance in its own different world, so we work with documents that specify the costumes and the props to come up with graphics and lighting that really set the scene.

'Sometimes there's a really specific idea

from the start. For example, if there is a Mamma Mia!-themed track, the reference is a Greek Island, so we know it's going to be on a beach and there will be a lot of blue-and-white buildings in the background. But if it's a pop song, they might want more abstract graphics, so it's more about shapes and movement, rather than any particular place.

'A brief might be as simple as "graphics need to be fun", which is open to interpretation. So we listen to the music, look at what else is in that week's show and find inspiration from somewhere.'

Having decided on a scene, David designs a graphic using 3D software, creating, for example, a building and then layering further images to add context.

'We can add different skies behind the building, we can add rain in front of the buildings and we can keep adding layers to get different effects,' he says. 'The good thing is that we can easily add extra layers if the dance requires a change. So if we want a slightly different look for the chorus to the verse, we can add a layer that is faster or brighter.'

Although the scenery lasts for the whole 90-second routine, David reveals his graphics actually run on a 12-second loop. So he may design one 12-second section for the verse, another for the chorus and separate loops for the floor projection and side screens.

'Each routine can take anything between an hour and five hours, on average, to create. A slow ballad that doesn't really change up, I can finish in an hour, but a song that changes tempo or a medley, like the Nile Rodgers group dance at the start of series 16, needs a lot more looks in it. Not only was it a medley of four different hits, it was also shot in two different locations, outside Broadcasting House and in the

Strictly studio. Each song had to have its own look to match the music, but the whole performance needed to feel cohesive. We ended up using the neon batons and variations of the mirror columns in the graphics for both locations.'

As the whole concept of the dance – wardrobe, props, hair and make-up – doesn't come together until dress rehearsal on Saturday, the two Davids and their talented teams are always prepared for last-minute changes.

'The graphics are signed off on Thursday night for that weekend's show and the lighting is led by the graphics,' says David Bishop. 'We consult with the producer about the colour palette that will complement the costumes, but quite often we will turn up to rehearsals and what we've talked about and rehearsed independently needs to change when it comes together.

'There's a great deal of variation in what people describe as red, for example. So we might have planned a lighting scheme that complemented fire-engine red, but when the costume is finally on, it turns out to be more rose red. But with new technology, these things have become easy to change quickly.'

When it comes to graphics, David Newton is also geared up for last-minute tweaks. 'It's very unusual that I'm still on version one of the graphic by the time we get to Saturday,' he says. 'Some will be major colour changes, because the running order of the show has changed, or because a concept isn't working, but some will be small changes, to improve and polish it.

'The Friday rehearsals are the first time that everyone has seen the ideas come together, so inevitably we see it and think, "I could improve that." We never make anything during the week thinking that it will be the final product. We go into rehearsals knowing we are probably only halfway there.'

Even as the dance is being performed on the live show, David Bishop is tweaking and perfecting.

'Dave Newton designs the content, but I run the media servers, so I can manipulate his graphics, I can change the colours and scale, I can position things and I get to cue when things happen, like fireworks.'

With technology advancing all the time, the *Strictly* studio is constantly being updated and, this year, the lighting has one major difference.

'The lights in previous years have moved and changed colour, but we could only choose from seven basic colours. With the new rig, we will be able to make any colour we want by mixing it inside the light, live,' says David Bishop.

'Within the light there are pieces of glass, in cyan, magenta and yellow, which move by remote control, meaning you can mix to make any colour.

'It will be fantastic and will add theatricality, because we can cross fade from one colour to another, rather than it being on or off, red, green or blue.'

While graphic designer David Newton says he has seen a huge improvement in both the speed and resolution of the screens since he started on the show in 2011, he is looking to the future – and to one particular advance.

'What we're hoping to do in the future is more real-time graphics, where the dancers can manipulate the graphics in real time, live,' he says. 'The technology is not quite there yet, and if we introduced it now it would be like going from a film to watching a video game, but that's the next leap forward.'

Sports presenter Mike Bushell would love to walk away with the Glitterball in December . . . because some fans already think he's won it.

'I get confused with Chris Hollins, who won in 2009,' he says. 'I've had kids walk up to me and say: 'Congratulations on winning *Strictly*,' and ask for a selfie. Now if I don't win, I'll finally be able to say, 'Chris Hollins was a lot better than me.''

Both Chris Hollins and Ore Oduba have come from being sports journalists on the *BBC Breakfast* couch to win the trophy and Mike is hoping to make it a hat-trick.

'Two of my colleagues have won *Strictly* so there is a lot of pressure,' he says. 'I'm probably 15 or 20 years older than they were at the time and Chris was a real sportsman before that. He played cricket at the MCC and played football at a decent level as well. But my BBC colleagues Carol Kirkwood and Naga Munchetty also did it and said 'Please just go and enjoy it, put a smile on your face and have fun'.

'I think it's a case of enjoying the ride for as long as it lasts. Every week is a bonus and I just want to embrace the journey and the *Strictly* family.'

Born in Yorkshire, Mike trained in drama and television at the University of Winchester and was a member of the National Youth theatre before changing direction and moving into journalism. After learning the ropes on local newspapers, he got his first broadcasting job in 1990, as a trainee reporter on BBC Radio Solent. He later moved to *South East Today* before landing a job as sports reporter on *BBC Breakfast*.

Although a keen football player and runner, Mike says dancing is proving one of the 'most extreme physical sports there is.'

'I am under no illusion as to how physical this is,' he says. 'I've tried over 500 different sports, some of them very extreme but this is right up there and takes the biscuit in terms of the physical demand and mental demands. There are muscles I never knew I had suddenly appearing, saying hello and hurting a little bit.

'It's not just your legs moving, not just your hips; it's your hands, your posture, your head, your face, your smile, your eyes – it's everything. There are few other sports that do that so for me this is the ultimate sporting challenge.'

While Mike takes running marathons in his stride, dancing is not something he currently lists among his skills.

'At a disco I like to jump up and down or link arms with people to "Come On Eileen" at the end of an evening,' he says. In terms of dancing ability I am right at the beginning.'

Mike thinks that having plenty of energy and enthusiasm will be the strengths he brings to the floor, and says he's planning to put in '100 percent and 100 hours a week' into training with partner Katya Jones.

'Maybe the faster dances might suit me better as I might be able to mask some of my technical deficiencies,' he says. 'I think I'll prefer the Charleston or the Jive because you can jump up and down. I got married at the end of May and we danced to "The Sun is Shining" which is quite fast. I might be able to get away with footwork if it seems like a fast blur.'

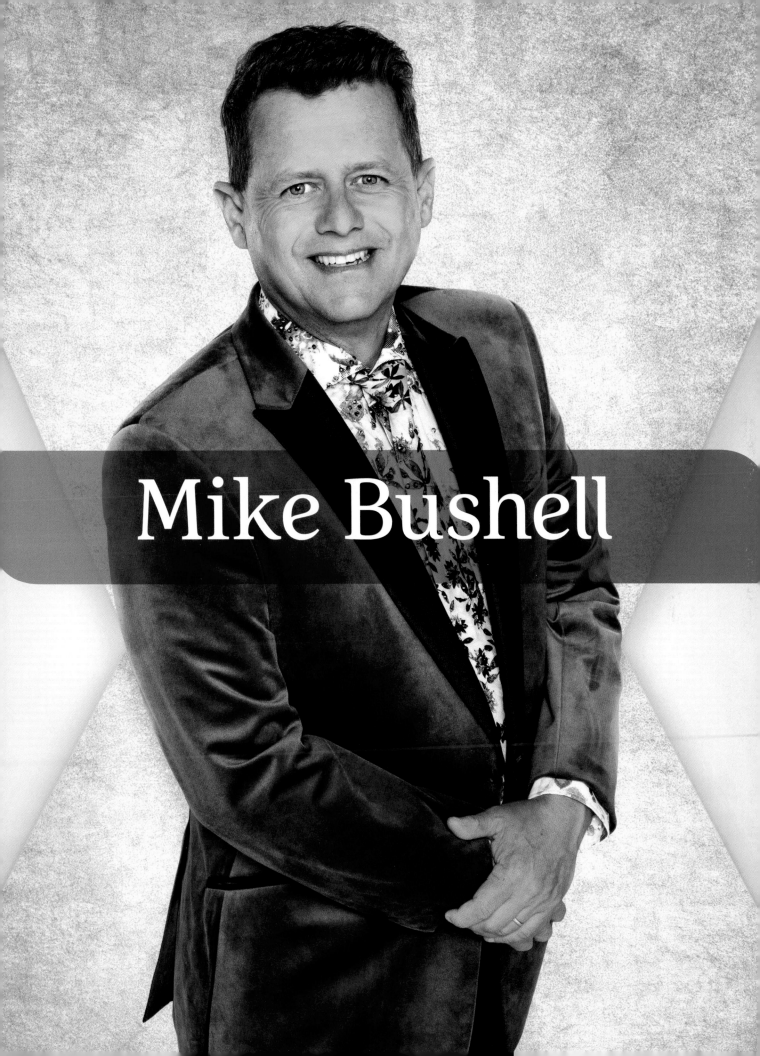

Mike Bushell

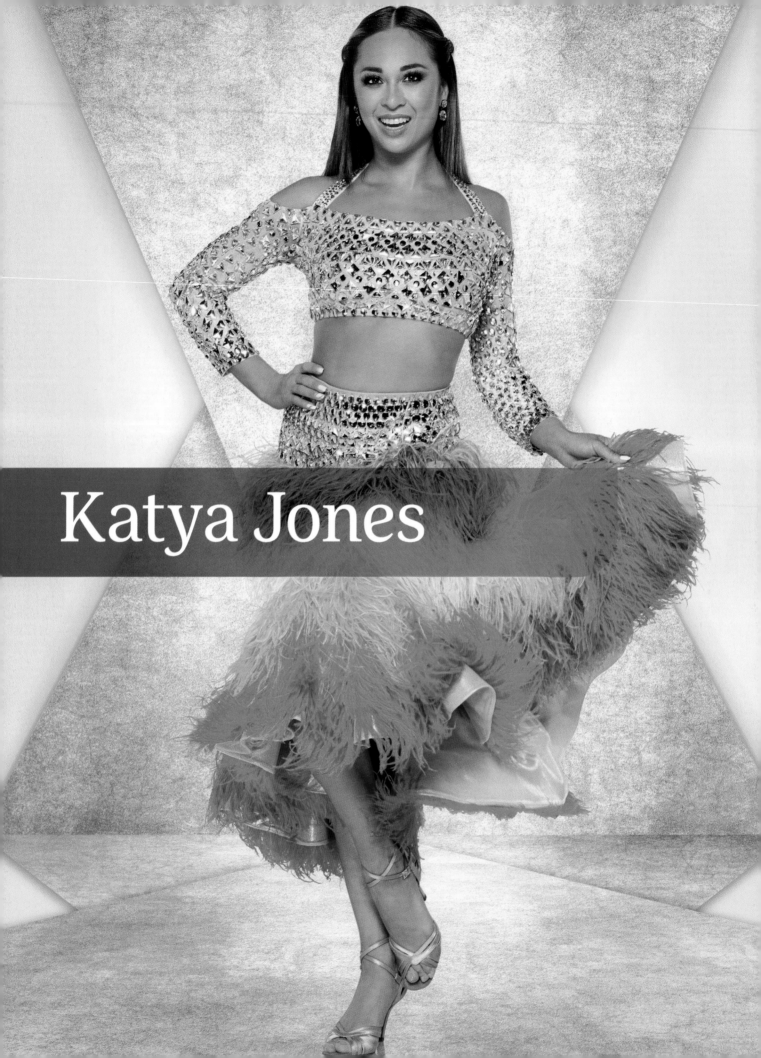

Katya Jones

Former *Strictly* champ Katya Jones is dragging Mike Bushell off his BBC *Breakfast* couch to put a twinkle in his toes this year. But the Russian pro thinks Mike might have a job reining in his enthusiasm.

'Mike is just lovely and so much fun,' she says. 'He's so excited, bouncing off the walls, so I'm over the moon.

'If anything, he sometimes has a bit too much energy which I will need to tame or, at least, direct in the right places. But he's looking forward to dancing and learning properly so that's really good.'

Katya was born in Saint Petersburg and started dancing at the age of six, training in gymnastics as well as ballroom and Latin American. In 2008, Katya met Neil Jones in Blackpool and they began dancing together. They became three-time World Amateur Latin Champions before turning professional and, in 2015, they became the World Professional Latin Showdance Champions. They are also four times undefeated British National Professional Champions.

Katya's first year on *Strictly*, in 2016, saw an unforgettable partnership with Ed Balls and she followed that with a win, steering Joe McFadden to victory. Last year she danced with Seann Walsh who was eliminated on week six.

'I've been very lucky because all the celebrities, as students, have been absolutely fantastic,' she says. 'I always want to give them a dance to remember. So the moment with Ed was Gangnam Style, with Joe it was the Argentine Tango and then, last year it was *The Matrix* Paso Doble. I'm really hoping that, when Mike has finished his experience, he'll have a *Strictly* dance he can be proud of for the rest of his life.'

As usual, Katya is raring to get going on her choreography and says Mike is open to trying anything she throws at him.

'Mike was a big fan of Ed and of what he represented on *Strictly*,' she says. 'And he's very excited. When he when he was paired with me, he said 'You've got all these ideas. I can't wait to do them.' And that's a great thing, knowing that he's open for anything, he's ready to embrace the whole *Strictly* experience and trust me. I've already come up with some ideas. It's going be good.'

As Mike has taken a break from BBC *Breakfast* they plan to put in as much training time as possible.

'Mike is fully committed to *Strictly* and he's become a fulltime dancer!' says Katya. He wants to be good and he knows we need work, so the more hours we put in the better outcome it will be.

'He's a Dad dancer and that's the only type of dancing he has done so he's a blank canvas. But he's just going to throw himself into it he doesn't have any dance experience, but I can make something out of him.'

After dancing her way to a Glitterball trophy two years ago, Katya is keen to make it a pair.

'My Glitterball sits on my piano in my living room, so I see it every day,' she says. 'They let me have the cue card, which they gave to Tess to announce the winners, so that's framed and the trophy stands next to it. The memories and the sentimental value is enormous, every time I look at it I still get emotional. The trophy is like a little motivation ball, I look at it and think 'it would be nice to do that again!''

Rylan Clark-Neal

Fan favourite Zoe Ball is now in her eighth year of presenting *Strictly*'s week-day spin-off, but this year a new face will be joining *It Takes Two* to make the show extra special. Rylan Clark-Neal is taking over presenting duties on Mondays and Tuesdays, and both he and Zoe will be the gracing the sofa on Fridays.

Rylan – who took over Zoe's Saturday show on Radio 2 when she moved to a daily slot – can't wait to 'bring some mischief to the *Strictly* bubble'.

'I'm really excited,' he says. 'I'm looking forward to getting my big old teeth stuck into the show, getting back into my spin-off world and immersing myself in *Strictly*, living and breathing it. More importantly, I love Zoe, so I can't wait to be working alongside her properly, rather than at arm's length. We've been involved in projects together but not hosting the same show, so I'm especially excited for the Friday show. The Friday show is fun because you have more guests and it's an hour, so it's more like a party.'

A model from the age of 16, Rylan appeared in *John Bishop's Britain* and won the modelling show *Signed* by Katie Price before finding nationwide fame as a finalist on *The X Factor*, in 2012. The following year, he won *Celebrity Big Brother,* which led to a presenting role on the sister show *Big Brother's Bit on the Side*. He also became a regular presenter on ITV's *This Morning*.

The 30-year-old from Essex says he has always wanted to compete on the *Strictly* dance floor, but presenting duties on *Big Brother* meant the timing was never right. 'I'd love to have done it, but it's always been impossible,' he says. 'Now the first year I am able to do it, I find myself hosting *It Takes Two* instead.'

Even so, Rylan is no stranger to the *Strictly* studio, having regularly supported *This Morning* colleague Ruth Langsford when she competed in 2017. And last year he popped up in the Clauditorium to announce the terms and conditions.

'The atmosphere is amazing and that comes through on the telly as well,' he says.

'There are not many shows where the way it feels to be in the studio comes across on screen. And the atmosphere backstage is really friendly, so I am thrilled to be joining the family.'

While he may be a new addition to *Strictly*, the TV host is very familiar with its home at Elstree Studios – as the *Big Brother* house was next door to the main stage. 'I used to bump into the *Strictly* lot all the time,' he says. 'I know all the pros, I know Tess and Claudia and all the production team, so it's really

all come together. Even though I'm the new boy, I pretty much know everybody, which is wonderful.'

As many who saw him on *The X Factor* will know, Rylan loves to dance and modestly confesses, 'I can definitely move my hips, let's put it that way.' But he's a novice when it comes to ballroom and Latin – and he hopes *It Takes Two* will rectify that.

'I'm sure I'll be put through my paces,' he says. 'I love watching Ian Waite when he teaches the dances, so I'm nervous and excited at the same time for that. I'm going to need to learn a full routine by the end of the series.'

To date, one of his favourite dances was Ann Widdecombe being 'dragged around the floor' in the Paso Doble, but there are a few other dance memories that stand out for Rylan.

'Caroline Flack and Debbie McGee were both absolutely breathtaking to watch,' he says. 'But the sight of Ruth dressed as a witch coming down on a broomstick will stay with me forever!' Not one to shy away from a flamboyant look, Rylan is looking forward to chats with the wardrobe department, as well as trying out the tanning booth. 'I've got several spray tans written into my contract,' he jokes. 'Every week!'

Catherine Tyldesley says her former *Coronation Street* stars are happy she's finally pulling on her dancing shoes – because she's *Strictly*'s number one fan.

'I don't think my Corrie friends were surprised that I'm taking part,' she explains. 'Every year when *Strictly*'s on, it's all I can talk about. They know it's my favourite show. 'Everyone has been so supportive and so excited. I don't think there's anybody I know who doesn't like *Strictly*. It's such a huge part of our year, we can't wait for it to start. All my friends and family are the same so everyone's thrilled.'

Catherine was born and raised in Greater Manchester and, after leaving school. Trained at the Birmingham School of Speech and Drama. In 2011, she landed the role of Eva Price in Coronation Street becoming a firm favourite with soap fans until her emotional departure in 2017. A talented singer, Catherine admits she played hooky when it came to dance lessons at drama school.

'I never had the confidence to take part in the dance classes – often I'd avoid them completely,' she says. 'I was a lot bigger than I am now and I just didn't enjoy it. My old dance teacher was very surprised when she heard I was doing this show. But I want to prove to myself I can do it and I want to learn a new skill. I'm in complete awe of what dancers can do.'

Although she is keen to get to the final, and try every dance, there's one particular routine that she's not looking forward to. 'I'm dreading – and I mean absolutely dreading – the Charleston,' she says. 'It's so hard. Before the launch show we did a basic run through of each dance for two minutes and when we did the Charleston, it's just impossible.

'I tried to show my mum and honestly, she was crying laughing. I was saying, 'Mum! Is it not even a bit right?''

Catherine hopes dance partner Johannes Radebe will be 'patient and supportive' as she'll be dancing outside her comfort zone. While she admits she's nervous about waiting in the wings and hearing her name, she is not afraid of the judges' comments – and even welcomes Craig's critique.

'Every year when I watch the show, because I'm a huge fan, and I agree with everything they say – including Craig,' she says. He's always right. He is always constructive and when you look at the dance, I always think 'yeah I get it.' So I just have to take on board what they're saying and hopefully implement it.'

Being a self-confessed 'girly girl', Catherine can't wait to see what sequins and sparkles the costume department come up with every week.

'The dresses are amazing,' she says. 'Behind the dresses it's like scaffolding, holding everything together. The costume team whip them up so fast and they have literally have hundreds to make. I can't wait to get glammed up every week. Hopefully even if my dancing's bad, my dress will look great!'

Catherine's biggest fan will be son Alfie, who will be staying up to watch her every Saturday night.

'He's only four but he loves it,' she says. 'He can't wait. He's been watching all the old dances on YouTube. He's obsessed with the Disney and Harry Potter dances. He'll watch each dance again and again. I'm going to get him a sparkly waistcoat.'

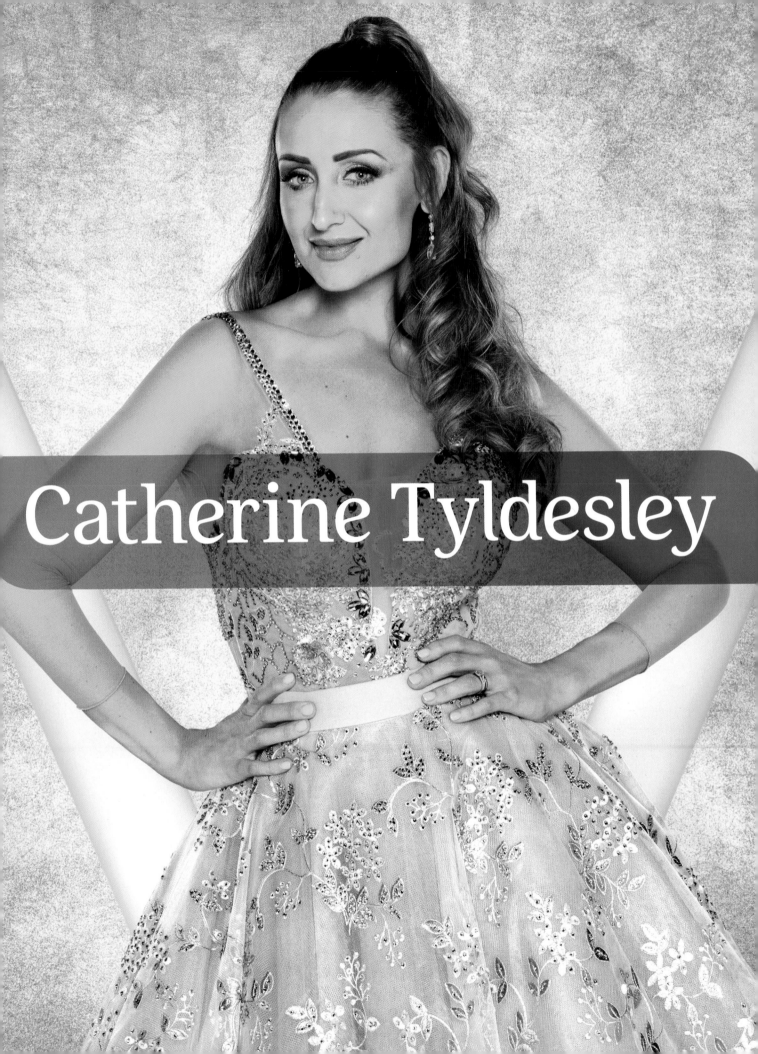

Catherine Tyldesley

Johannes Radebe

South African dancer Johannes Radebe joined the *Strictly* pros last year but this is the first time he has been paired with a celebrity. And he's already getting on like a house of fire with *Coronation Street* star Catherine Tyldesley.

'I am so lucky,' he says. 'Catherine is such a nice lady and we have been having such a laugh. It is so great to be partnered with her. I think I'm the luckiest of all of them.'

He and Catherine were the first to be paired at the Launch Show and Johannes was taken by surprise to hear his name. But I thought 'whoever I get I'll be very happy' because it's my first time having a partner when I found out that I got Catherine, I just went, 'Yes!''

'We are well paired and I think in a ballroom frame, she will look fantastic in ballroom hold' he says. I think our strides will complement one another and she will be my perfect match.

'Also I love her feet. She's got dancer's feet, with a nice point. She also has an outgoing personality, she's not shy and she's a good actor, so she can take up the character. I'm really excited that I don't have to worry about her performance skills. I don't know about remembering the choreography, but she's willing to work hard and I'll be with her every step of the way. I said to her 'This is our journey and we make the rules.''

There was one small thing that Johannes noticed in the group rehearsals, however. 'Catherine twirled once and got dizzy!' he explains. 'I think we're going have to sort out that dizziness as quickly as possible – especially if we get to do a Viennese Waltz.'

Although it's his first year competing on *Strictly Come Dancing*, Johannes has reached the final of the South African version twice. Before that, he performed with the Afro Arimba Dance Company, as well as being a two-time Professional South African Latin Champion and three-time South African Amateur Latin Champion.

Joining the UK show was a long term ambition and he says he had an 'amazing time' in his first year.

'When I got the phone call inviting me over to be part of the *Strictly* family, for me, that was everything,' he says. 'I've always aspired to be part of this show so last year was incredible. I got to work with the most amazing choreographers, on the most amazing group dances and I got to dance among the most fabulous artists. It was the most incredible journey of my life.'

Watching from the sidelines also gave Johannes an extra insight into the challenges ahead.

I'm prepared,' he says. Everybody wants to be a *Strictly Come Dancing* champion and nobody walks into the competition thinking I just want to make it to week three. It is natural to want to win. That's what I plan on doing. Me and my partner, Catherine are going to give everyone a run for their money!'

The A–Z of *Strictly*

A is for American Smooth

The ballroom dance that brings Hollywood glamour to the dance floor can be a real showstopper. Introduced in series three, it can include steps from the Waltz, Viennese Waltz, Tango, Quickstep and Foxtrot, but, unlike all of these, only 40 per cent needs to be in hold. The rules now allow three lifts in the routine. Four celebrities have so far earned perfect scores for the dance – Ali Bastian, Natalie Gumede, Alexandra Burke and Ashley Roberts.

B is for Blackpool

Every year the whole *Strictly* party decamps to the home of ballroom dancing where the remaining couples get to compete in the grand surroundings of Blackpool Tower Ballroom. As well as providing a benchmark to aim for, the iconic venue has also played host to two *Strictly* finals, in 2004 and 2011. The ballroom was built in 1894 and the interior designed by Frank Matcham in the flamboyant style of Louis XV's Renaissance period. It boasts rich upholstery, stunning murals and crystal chandeliers, with gold leaf trimmings and, crucially, a sprung dance floor.

C is for Couple's Choice

Introduced in series 16, the Couple's Choice round gives dancers the opportunity to choose between three dance disciplines – Street/Commercial, Theatre/Jazz and Contemporary. For a full guide of this fantastic round see page 64.

D is for Dance-off

A permanent fixture of the competition since series 10, the dance-off gives the two couples who are bottom of the leader board one more chance to impress the judges and stay in the competition. After both have performed their dances for a second time, the judges vote on which couple they want to save. If the vote is evenly split, the head judge has the casting vote.

E is for Elstree

The Hertfordshire studio has been home to *Strictly Come Dancing* since 2013, when it moved from BBC Television Centre in West

London. The Saturday and Sunday shows are filmed at the George Lucas Stage, where the iconic Star Wars films were shot.

F is for Fleckerl

This dance step, often mentioned by the *Strictly* judges, translates from the German as 'small spot'. A standard step in the Viennese Waltz, it is a rotating step danced on the spot, either clockwise or counter-clockwise (natural or reverse) and over six bars. The fast spins on the spot can leave the novice dancer feeling a little dizzy.

G is for Glitterball Trophy

The glittering prize that every contestant wants to get their hands on was designed by prop-makers Keir and Louise Lusby in 2004. In series nine the base was replaced so that more winners' names could be engraved on the trophy. At the end of each series, the winning couple are given a mini version of the glitterball, which they keep.

H is for Heel Leads

The judges will often point out heel leads or toe leads, particularly if a dancer uses the wrong one! A heel lead is akin to walking, where the dancer puts the foot down heel first and then rolls through the foot as they transfer weight. For the toe lead, you start with the toe and back through to the heel. In general, forward steps in the ballroom standards (the Waltz, Tango, Foxtrot, Quickstep and Viennese Waltz) require heel leads, while in the Latin dances, you lead with the toe. Incidentally, it's almost impossible to lead with the heel on a backward step. Try it and you'll soon see why!

I is for International

Launched in the UK in 2004, *Strictly*'s format has gone on to wow audiences worldwide. Renamed *Dancing with the Stars* in most territories, it now has been licensed to 57 countries, from the US to Ukraine, Iceland to India and from Serbia to South Africa. In fact, there have been versions of the show across six of the seven continents.

J is for Judges

Firm but fair, the Fabulous Foursome have a wealth of dance experience between them and are there to help. With constructive criticism and praise the panel help the celebrities improve their techniques and their scores, and of course, are crucial to who is top and bottom of the leader board.

K is for Kicks and Flicks

As all *Strictly* aficionados know, the judges look for 'kicks and flicks' throughout any Jive. But what's the difference? A kick uses the whole leg in one movement, coming from the hip, as if kicking a ball. For a flick, the thigh is raised and then the movement comes from the knee, with toes pointing down towards the floor.

L is for Lifts

Lifts are against the rules in most of the dances, including the five classic Latin styles and five core ballroom dances, in which dancers must have one foot on the ground at all times. While the judges may have to penalise contestants for illegals lifts in a routine it can help to win the support of the fans at home. The exceptions are the American Smooth, Argentine Tango and Salsa, as well as the Couple's Choice dances and, of course, the Showdance.

M is for Music

There's no dancing without music, and for *Strictly* it has to be live. Music maestro Dave Arch spins his magic to come up with a 90-second arrangement for the song to be played by his wonderful orchestra on the night with vocals from the *Strictly* singers.

N is for New Yorker

A basic Cha-cha-cha step where the couple begins facing each other (open facing position), then turns 90 degrees with one hand in hold (open position), before returning to the centre and repeating to the other side.

O is for Orchestra

The *Strictly* orchestra is among the most versatile in the world, bringing everything from the big band sound to the most contemporary pop song to the dance floor and providing the perfect accompaniment to every dance routine. The core line-up consists of eight brass – three trumpets, two trombones and three saxophones – and a rhythm section of seven, including drums, percussion, bass, two guitarists and two keyboard players. Multi-talented band leader Dave Arch then adds piano, keyboard and the occasional turn on the guitar.

P is for Props

From cannons and coffins to full side-byside dressing rooms, imaginative props help to set the scene and tell the story of each dance. Props designer Catherine Land and set designer Patrick Doherty often have less than a week to come up with the stage furniture for the dances and, as well as looking amazing, they have to be very portable – as the four-strong props team have just 90 seconds between dances to whip them on and off.

Q is for Quickstep

At 50 bars a minute, compared to 30 for the Waltz, the Quickstep lives up to its name and proves a favourite ballroom dance with both contestants and viewers. Originating in the 1920s, when bands upped the pace of music they played in dance halls, the dance incorporates elements of the Foxtrot and Charleston. A perfect score has been bagged by four *Strictly* celebs – Lisa Snowdon, Ricky Whittle, Pamela Stephenson and Harry Judd – and in series 13 a Quickstep-a-thon was won by Helen George and Aljaž Škorjanec.

R is for Rumba

The dance of love originated in Cuba but became a popular ballroom dance after being introduced in the United States in the 1930s. A slow, fluid but highly technical dance, steps are taken with bent knee, which, when straightened, causes the hips to sway in what is known as the 'Cuban motion'. Rumba remains the only the dance that has never been a awarded a perfect 40 by the judges. Although some have come close with Kara and Artem, Rachel and Vincent and Aliona and Jay all receiving 39 for their Rumbas.

S is for Showdance

One of the highlights of the Final, this is the couples' chance to rip up the rule books and put in as many lifts and tricks as they like to wow the judges and the audience. Anything goes. The Showdance was not scored by the judges in series two to six, but since then it has garnered nine perfect scores.

T is for Ten

The highest paddle of them all is what every dancer strives for and many now achieve. In total, the judges have awarded a total of 768 perfect 10s, with Alexandra Burke and Ashley Roberts getting the most, at 32 each. The number of routines that have scored all four 10s currently stands at 61.

U is for Underdog

Part of the magic of *Strictly* is that the fans at home get to vote for their favourites on the show. *Strictly* fans love to see a contestant progress and learn a new skill. With the guidance of their pro partners, complete novices often triumph in the Final and that's what makes the show so unpredictable – and so exciting.

V is for Vote

The *Strictly* voting system puts you the viewer in charge. After the judges give their verdicts, the couples are ranked in order of score and points awards accordingly. When the public vote is counted, the couples are again ranked and awarded points and the two scores added together. And in the Final, it's only the viewer's vote that counts – meaning *Strictly* fans always choose the champ.

W is for Wardrobe

Putting the sparkle into *Strictly*, the talented wardrobe team, led by Vicky Gill, work right up to the wire to perfect their amazing creations. While each look is weeks in the planning, final alterations and embellishments are still being completed on the day of the shows, sometimes with minutes to spare. With almost 150 couple dances per series, plus professional dances, that's no mean feat.

X is for Xmas

The festive period sees the main show coming to a spectacular crescendo, with the Final, but when it's over there's still one present left under the tree for avid fans – the Christmas Special. First aired in 2004, the Christmas bonus sees a mixture of *Strictly* stars and new contestants battling it out with a dance to a seriesal song to win the glitterstar trophy. Previous contestants include Vince Cable, Elaine Paige and Fabrice Muamba, and winners include Charlie Brooks, Melvin Odoom and Ali Bastian.

Y is for You

Strictly Come Dancing fans are what the show is all about, after all. Over 12 million tuned in to the Finals in recent years and thousands have turned out to watch the live tour over the last ten years. We salute you.

Z is for Zoe

Zoe Ball fell in love with *Strictly* as a series three finalist and has been unable to stay away since. She has competed in two Christmas Specials with dance partner Ian Waite, and as the host of *It Takes Two* she now gets to keep *Strictly* devotees ticking over in the long wait for the next Saturday show.

YouTube star Saffron Barker has found a staunch supporter in her nan, who couldn't be prouder that her granddaughter is competing on the show.

'When she was younger my nan wanted to be a dancer but her family only had enough money to send one of her sisters to dance classes,' she explains. 'So she has told me I'm living her dream, which is really special. My nan has been calling me every single day – she's cried a lot and told me she's very proud. She keeps telling me to sing the song I Have Confidence from The Sound of Music to boost my confidence.

'The reaction has been crazy. It's been even bigger than I expected and the support has been incredible.'

Brighton-born Saffron launched her online career at the age of 14, releasing a cover of the Mark Ronson and Bruno Mars hit Uptown Funk with girl group Born2Blush. When the band folded, she set up her own YouTube channel which took off with the release of her comedic Types of Boyfriends video in 2016. The clip has since amassed over nine million views and Saffron now has two million subscribers on YouTube and two million Instagram followers.

At 19, she's the youngest of this year's celebrities but she also boasts the most impressive dance injury.

'I pulled every ligament in my leg while I was dancing in my bedroom!' she reveals. 'Genuinely, I was just completely messing around. I don't even know what we were dancing to – probably Justin Bieber. We were dancing around, I sat down and I just couldn't get up. I had to stay in hospital for three days.'

Saffron briefly attended Jazz and Modern Dance classes when she was eight but, other than that, she is a dance novice. She's looking forward to the ballroom dances but says she's nervous about the Cha Cha Cha. 'Moving your hips – no! I do want to do something sassy though, like the Paso Doble. 'I'm looking forward to learning how to dance and trying on the dresses. It's an incredible thought that I could learn such an amazing skill while doing a TV show. It will be a challenge and I'm nervous about the live shows. Strictly will be a world away from the YouTube life I am used to.'

Saffron is following in the footsteps of fellow influencer Joe Sugg, who made the final, and he has been voicing his support. 'Joe Sugg told me to just enjoy the moment,' she says. 'But it'll be my mum who I look to for advice. I'm so close to her.

There's no one I trust more than my mum; I can always count on her.'

In fact, her mum was the only one she told before her name was officially announced and they devised a secret code word for Strictly.

'My mum and I referred to it as 'The Dream' when we were out in public before everyone else knew, as it really was a dream,' says Saffron. 'I have always wanted to do the show. I can't believe it's actually happening.'

Saffron Barker

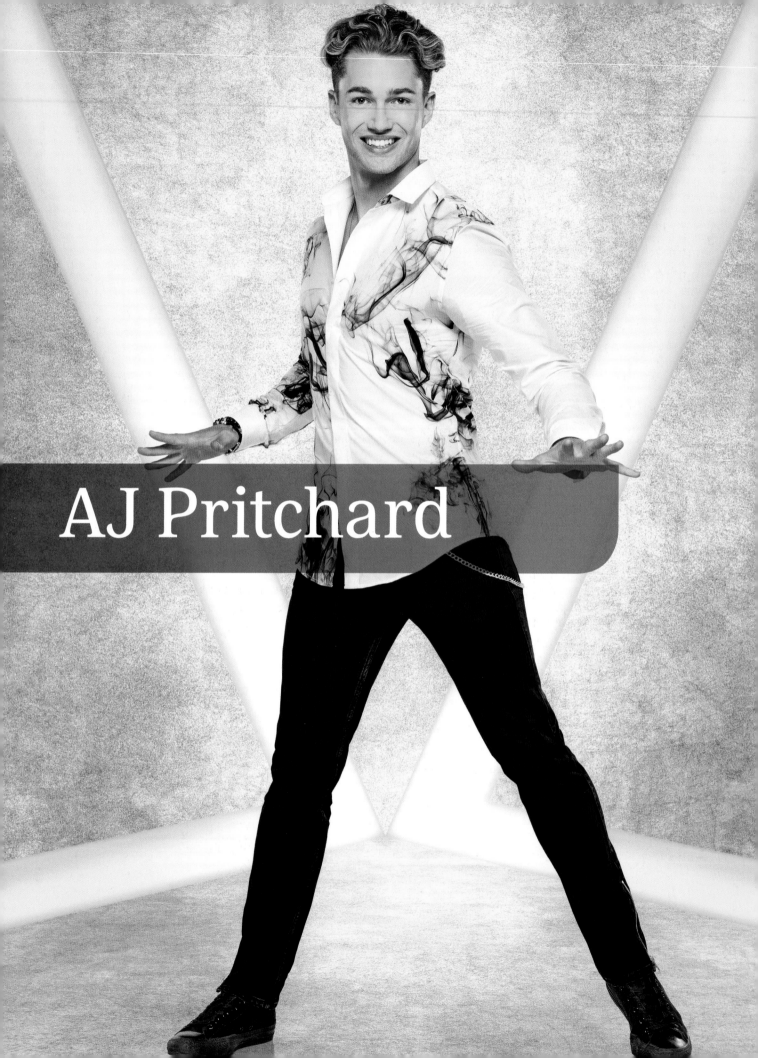

AJ Pritchard

For the last three years, AJ Pritchard has been within touching distance of the Final, making it as far as the Semi-finals with Claudia Fragapane, Mollie King and Lauren Steadman. But this year, dancing with Saffron Barker, he's feeling even luckier.

'Saffron has cleared her diary and wants to train as many hours as possible, so she is a dream.'

The secret of success in *Strictly* is taking every week as though it is your last and enjoying it. But I have planned so many Finals and not danced them – I can't do that to myself again!'

'Honestly, on the night of the Launch Show I had no idea,' he recalls. 'When my name was called I screamed and punched the air. I was going to do a bit of a trick with my legs, but they went to jelly. So when I walked over to her I just hugged her. I was so happy and we're having so much fun.'

Born in Stoke-on-Trent, AJ was a lover of extreme sports such as snowboarding and mountain boarding before a broken arm prompted him to swap the slopes for the dance floor. His parents, who ran a local dance school, paired him with Chloe Hewitt and together they became National Youth Latin Champions three years running, as well as European Youth Latin Champions. He joined *Strictly* in 2016 and last year he danced with Paralympic gold medallist Lauren.

'For Lauren, it was more than just the *Strictly* journey,' he says. 'It was about changing the perception of people at home. 'This is going to be a very different year, but it's always rewarding for me as a teacher, whoever I get. All my partners have become good friends. From going for a Sunday roast with Mollie to supporting both Olympians, Claudia and Lauren, and wishing them well for their next championships, we all stay in touch.'

As they embark on their own dance adventure, AJ says Saffron is bursting with enthusiasm and is a real superfan. 'People say they watch *Strictly*, but she loves it!' he says. 'She knows everything about it, and it's really nice having somebody that's grown up watching the show.

'Saffron's mentality is always, "Yes, I'll give it a go." We may have to draw the energy back a bit, but it's much easier to tell someone to do less than to try and push them. It's fresh, youthful energy.'

Vlogger Saffron has wasted no time in getting AJ into her YouTube videos.

'Saffron got me involved straight away,' laughs AJ. 'And I'm happy to be in her vlogs as much as she wants.'

The young pro has been taking up a few extra challenges of his own in recent years, too – competing in *Celebrity Masterchef* and, last year, winning *Celebrity Hunted*. 'Anything with adrenaline or pressure is what I seem to be drawn to,' he says. 'So, for me, I'm keen to up the adrenaline by making it to the Final this year!'

Smoke & Mirrorballs

It was 'Love at First Sight' for *Strictly* fans when superstar Kylie Minogue kicked off series 17 at the red-carpet event. After the professionals took to the stage, a huge gold mirrorball spun round to reveal the Australian pop star – who opened the show with a medley of hits.

Set designer Patrick Doherty says Kylie couldn't have been happier. 'She loved it,' he explains. 'We showed Kylie how it would look, with her choreographer standing in for her, and when she saw the mirrorball turn round, she started jumping up and down. She thought it was very exciting.'

This year's event moved from its previous setting of New Broadcasting House in Central London to Television Centre (TVC) in West London – the original home of *Strictly*.

Despite its name, there was no actual red carpet. 'Every year, the event gets bigger and bigger,' says executive producer Sarah James. 'When we watched last year's Launch Show, it looked so amazing, and we thought, "Why don't we do more?" As soon as we knew we had Kylie, we wanted more of a concert feel, with 18 pros dancing on a big stage outside TVC, with Kylie. What an amazing way to kick off the series!'

After the glitterball, there was more magic – when the stage rose up by 1.5 metres, with smoke and coloured light pouring from underneath. The impressive scene was once again all the work of Patrick and his team, who spent months planning the complicated build.

'In the middle of the stage, we had a hydraulic lift that moves a section up and down, so we designed it around that,' he reveals.

That was then covered with a reflective gloss studio flooring, and lines of LED lights, forming a diamond, were embedded in the stage. Huge trusses – metal structures that support the lighting – framed the extended stage, which radiated out from the centre.

'We wanted to embrace the fact that we were back at TVC and make a feature of the building,' says Patrick. 'So we used translucent elements, lighting with gaps, so that you could get colour and content but you could still see through to TVC.'

The huge mirrorball that Kylie stepped off reflected the new colours of the *Strictly* logo, and was built by a specialist company, using thousands of pieces of gold mirror glued onto a fiberglass shell, 2 metres in diameter. The whole thing was built on wheels so that it could quickly be whipped off the stage during Kylie's performance.

Patrick began to draw up plans in May, working with lighting director Dave Bishop. But on the scorching August bank holiday weekend, he and his team of 25 men – including four carpenters, four riggers, six lighting engineers and six stage builders – had just two days to construct it.

By the morning of the show, however, it was ready for Kylie to take to the stage and meet the dancers for rehearsals. Up until that point, Kylie and her dancers had been working on a routine choreographed by her team while liaising with *Strictly* choreographer Jason Gilkison, who came up with the pros' dance.

'By the time everybody gets there, they know what they're doing,' says Patrick. 'But it's a different set of parameters when you get on the stage. So, on the day, they all met and rehearsed together for the first time.' The event is the first glimpse of the celebs in all their sparkly glory, trying out a few moves, and it all went without a hitch.

'The celebrities were so enthusiastic and looked fantastic in their *Strictly* outfits,' says Sarah. 'It all looked fabulous.'

Which Pro is Which?

Psssst, want to know a secret? Our professional dancers have come up with some surprising facts about themselves to share with their loyal *Strictly* fans. To make it even more fun, we're asking you to guess which secret belongs to which pro. So how well do you know your favourite dancer?

1 'I sleep hugging a big teddy bear – Sully from *Monsters, Inc*. He was a sweet present and became my hugging pillow.

2 'I have a double-jointed thumb'

3 'I worked at a bank for six years. I started working at a bank when I turned 18 to help out with my bills and pay for my car, while at the same time studying finance at university. I danced every other hour of the week that I was not at work or at university. I only stopped working at the bank when I got my "big dance break" and my professional dance career began.'

4 'I'm scared of heights and two years ago we did a Halloween group number when I was supposed to be flying down on a chandelier and I just couldn't do it, so someone else stepped in.'

5 'When I was three years old I cut chunks of my little sister's hair off with Crayola scissors. It was her first haircut!'

6 'If I hadn't pursued my dancing, I would have been a nurse – inspired by my wonderful aunt.'

7 'You'll often see me with a bunch of flowers as a prop, but I'm actually allergic to them so I steer well clear of them in real life.'

8 'I am obsessed with wrestling and I grew up being obsessed with The Rock (still am). As a kid, my fave was Bret "The Hitman" Hart. He used to pick out a kid in the audience to give his pink shades to, but when I went to see him live I was sat near the back. So my parents bought me some replica shades from the merchandise stand and I told everyone at school he gave them to me.'

9 'My first job was as a cashier at a supermarket in Queens.'

10 'I have six tattoos including one saying "woof" in pink for my dog'

11 'I can't ride a bicycle.'

12 'If I had not been a dancer, I would have been a farmer and worked in the vineyards in the countryside with my father.'

13 'I once had a broken toe and carried on dancing for six months before I found out!'

14 'I was a salesman at 17, working full time in a bed showroom and dancing in the evening.'

15 'I can't eat apples before midday. It's a strange thing, but munching an apple after 12 is totally fine, but if I have one before I feel physically ill'

16 'I won my country's under-13s Track and Field in the 300 metres at the age of 12, breaking the national record – and I held it for 10 years.'

17 'I'm a dab hand at sewing – and used to make my own competition dresses.'

18 'I am scared of cats. I can't even tell you the reason

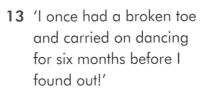

Emma Barton follows a long line of *EastEnders* stars who have danced up a storm on *Strictly* – including former champions Jill Halfpenny and Kara Tointon. And she's been quizzing her co-stars for tips after signing up for this year's line-up.

'A lot of them are saying to make sure you get plenty of massages, and I'm definitely happy doing that,' she reveals. 'Some said, "Don't forget the steps," which is helpful.

Jake Wood said, "If all else fails, just wiggle those hips." They've all been really supportive.'

The actress, who plays Honey Mitchell in the soap, says she is like a 'kid in a sweet shop' since coming on board and can't wait to swap her Minute Mart tabard for a bit of sparkle.

'I can't stop grinning,' she says. 'When I went onto the set for the first time I was thinking, "Oh my goodness, this is actually happening." It's just a little girl's dream to be dancing, dressing up, make-up, hair, feathers – bring it on!'

Hampshire-born Emma trained at the Guildford School of Acting. She joined *EastEnders* in 2005 and has played Honey, on and off, ever since.

'I haven't done any dancing or any sort of movement for about eight years, but I've got musicality,' she says. 'I've not trained specifically in dance, but from 18 I did three years of musical-theatre school, so I do know some of the basics. However, I was bottom of every dance class – that's a true fact – so it will be great to start again.'

When it comes to her favourite style of dance, Emma is looking to go back in time. 'We've only had a couple of hours to try a masterclass of all the different styles, so I'm not sure which will suit me best,' she says. 'But as a viewer I love watching the ballroom dances. I definitely don't think I was born in the right era, so I love the elegant vibe, the dresses, the hair – and the fact that they're slower might be helpful for me, too.'

As her parents are fans of the show, Emma is hoping she can make it to the iconic Tower Ballroom in Blackpool, so she can take them along to watch her dance.

'My mum and dad would be so proud if I got to Blackpool,' she says. 'But what will be will be. I'm just going to enjoy every minute and see what happens.'

The busy soap star will be fitting her training sessions around her filming commitments for EastEnders, but as both shows are shot at Elstree, she is confident she can pull it off.

'I'm not shy of working hard,' she says. 'You have just got to embrace it and go with it. There was no way I was going to say no to this. It's a once-in-a-lifetime opportunity. 'I am the biggest *Strictly* fan, so when the call came through, I thought, "Wow, that means I won't be sitting at home watching it, I'm actually going to be doing it!" 'It's the best. It's the classiest and just one of the most well-received shows that you could do. You're learning such an amazing craft from the best people in the business and you get to dress up in gorgeous costumes. It was a no-brainer.'

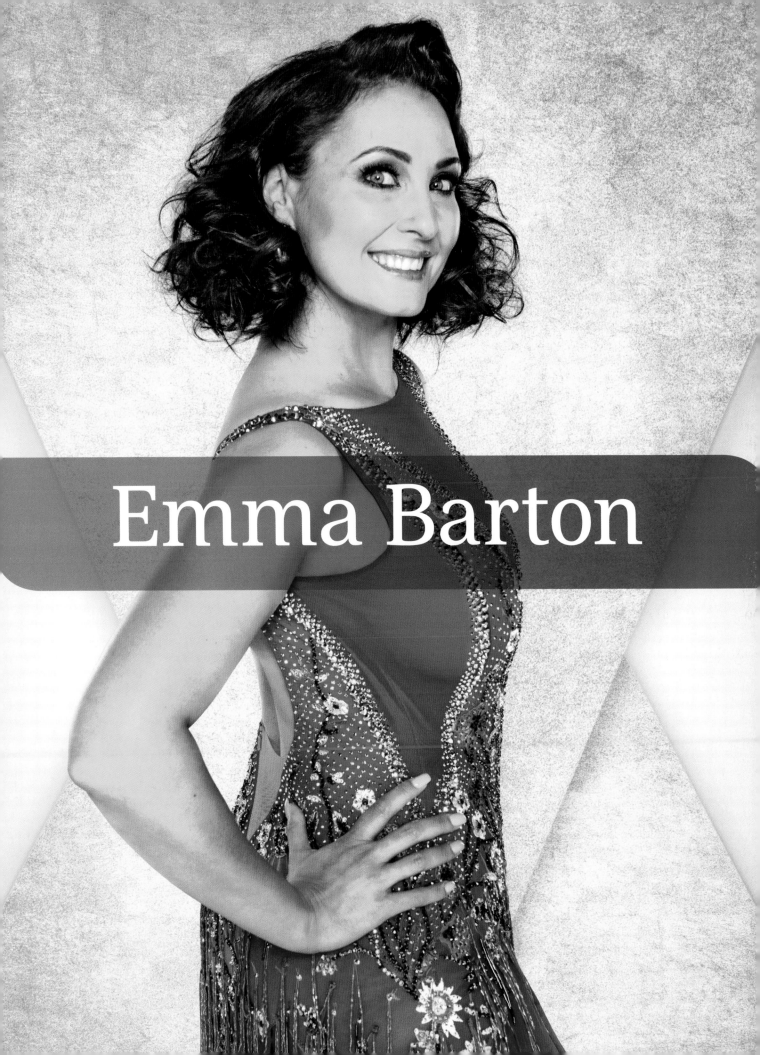

Emma Barton

Anton Du Beke

Ballroom king Anton du Beke has been lighting up the dance floor since series one and is the only original professional dancer left on the show. Yet to pick up a glitterball, Anton thinks that this could be his year, as he's excited to be dancing with *EastEnders* star Emma Barton

When paired on the Launch Show, the *Strictly* joker quipped, 'So this is what it feels like! Book me in till Christmas.'

'I couldn't be more excited,' he says. 'First impressions? She's brilliant! She knocked off the first routine in days. I couldn't be more delighted.'

Anton was born in Sevenoaks, Kent, to a Spanish mother and Hungarian father. Boxing and football were his favourite sports until he came to dancing at the relatively late age of 14. He trained in contemporary, jazz, ballet and modern theatre dance until, inspired by his idol Fred Astaire, he decided to specialise in ballroom.

In 1998 and 1999, Anton and dance partner Erin Boag won the New Zealand Championship. The pair joined *Strictly* for the first series in 2004 and Erin left in 2010. Since first waltzing onto the *Strictly* dance floor with Lesley Garrett, Anton has danced with 16 celebrities, including Lesley Joseph, Ruth Langsford and Jerry Hall, and picked up a total of 2,064 points from the judges. He has also gone down in *Strictly* legend for producing some of its most iconic moments – from Ann Widdecombe's Titanic Rumba and

flying Tango to Judy Murray's 'Cruella de Vil' American Smooth.

In 2015, Anton finally made it to the Final for the first time in 12 series, with Radio 3 presenter Katie Derham. Last year, Anton danced with Susannah Constantine and, sadly, they were the first couple to leave.

'We clicked instantly,' says Anton. 'It was like we'd known each other for 100 years. It was just all too brief, but I had the most fabulous time with Susannah, we had enormous amounts of fun.'

As the show's veteran, Anton says *Strictly* is a unique experience for both teacher and pupil. 'The unique thing about the show is the fact that it's a shared experience,' he says. 'In a normal world, we would teach somebody to dance, then we'd send them off and they'd go and dance with a partner. We would never dance with a student.'

Despite his growing list of memorable dances, one of Anton's favourite memories from the show doesn't involve his celebrity partners but singing and dancing to 'Me and My Shadow' with his own entertainment icon, Bruce Forsyth. 'That's one of the highlights of my life. To do something with your hero is so special. I feel honoured I had the opportunity to do that.'

As he enters his 17th series, fan-favourite Anton still has one or two ambitions he'd like to achieve. 'I'd like to get my first 10,' he says. 'I'd like to make it to the Final and I'd like to win!'

Zoe Ball

With a daily radio show on BBC2, Zoe Ball is handing over some of her *It Takes Two* duties to Rylan Clark-Neal this year.

But even at her busiest, the former Strictly contestant didn't want to waltz off the programme altogether. Instead Zoe will be gracing the ITT sofa on Wednesday and Thursday and joining Rylan on the hour long Friday show. 'I'm so excited,' she says. 'It comes around so quickly. It's like going back to school, returning to our little family. It's a joy.'

Zoe, who took over the show from Claudia Winkleman in 2011, can't wait to welcome the latest member of the ITT family 'I'm looking forward to working with Rylan a lot!' she says. 'He's certainly going to liven things up so it's going to be extra special this year.

'I met him in a lift once at ITV and completely fan girl-ed after him. I guess it was after *The X-Factor*, when he first started doing *Big Brother*. I just love him! I think he's going to be just fab. It also feels like it's meant to be – when I took over the *Breakfast Show* on Radio 2, Rylan took over my Saturday afternoon radio slot. You just know he's a great guy but also a complete scream. And as Rylan's so tall that I can wear a nice high heel!'

While Rylan has never competed on the show, Zoe is hoping that the *Strictly* professionals will be able to teach him a step or two on the show.

'I'd like to think we can get him dancing,' she says. 'I can definitely see Aljaž, Ian Waite and Anton teaching him. I think he'd be good at a Rumba or a Cha Cha Cha. Rylan's a great mover – we saw that on *The X Factor*.'

As well as getting to know her co-host, Zoe is keen to meet the new crop of *Strictly* hopefuls.

'There are so many of this year's celebrities that I was excited about,' she says. 'I love all of them and they will all become like my children. It's all looking very promising. 'I can't wait.'

Zoe, who danced her way to the Final with Ian Waite in series 3, still loves to dust off her dancing shoes on *It Takes Two*, whenever she gets the chance.

'When I get to dance with the pros I get a taste of the magic again,' she says. 'But I really just enjoy following the partnerships each year and becoming so obsessed with the show, so I can't wait for it all to start again.

'The studio's always full of mayhem but now I'm surrounded by tall handsome men – with Rylan, Ian Waite and Gethin Jones –it's not a bad place to be!'

Comedian Chris Ramsey says wife Rosie is thrilled he's taking part in *Strictly* because she has trouble dragging him on to the dance floor.

'When "Bones" by Michael Kiwanuka comes on the radio we will dance wherever we are because it was the first dance at our wedding,' he says. 'Other than that my standard move is my wife trying to get me up and me refusing to move. I won't even dance at weddings because I'm so bad so this will hopefully help.'

'I was looking forward to meeting Michelle Visage because my wife is a huge fan,' he says. 'As soon as Michelle was announced, I lost my wife's vote. 'My son is only three, so I'm not sure how much he'll take in. I want someone to film how he reacts to my first dance, but I have a feeling his first reaction will be 'Put Tom and Jerry on!' He will be confused at why the telly is on and it's not his favourite programme. He has been constantly singing the *Strictly* theme tune though because he's heard us watching clips on our phones. One day I'll catch it on camera!'

Born in South Shields, Chris's rise to fame began in 2010 when he took his stand up show, *Aggrophobic*, to the Edinburgh Fringe. Since then he has appeared on comedy panel shows including *Mock The Week*, *8 Out of 10 Cats Does Countdown* and *Celebrity Juice* as well as starring in the BBC2 sitcom *Hebburn*.

Chris says his family were surprised when he sprung the news he was taking part in *Strictly* – but his dad is now on a mission to get him fit for the dance floor.

'My family was like, 'Really? Can you dance? You can't dance! Are you sure?' he laughs. 'But then my dad turned into Mickey, the trainer from *Rocky*. He rings up and says, 'You done any runs? You need to do runs to get fit.' Honestly he's obsessed with making me fit.'

Secretly, however, Chris is keen to reach the peak of physical fitness.

'I'm looking forward to all of it but especially getting fit,' he says. 'Everyone says you get ripped. I've never been ripped. Ever. That would be great.

'I'm also looking forward to the spectacle of the whole thing; the live shows, the crowd, the costumes…'

Partnered with Karen Hauer, Chris is hoping she will be gentle with him.

'I'm a bit of a wimp,' he admits. 'I need someone to be nice to me. I also need someone who won't mind having their toes stood on.'

While the funnyman says he is taking the competition seriously, and is very competitive, his real goal is to learn to dance well enough to bust some moves in public.

'My dream in life is to challenge someone in a club or at a wedding to a dance off and win. This is the first step towards that dream – although I might have to take Karen with me to do it!'

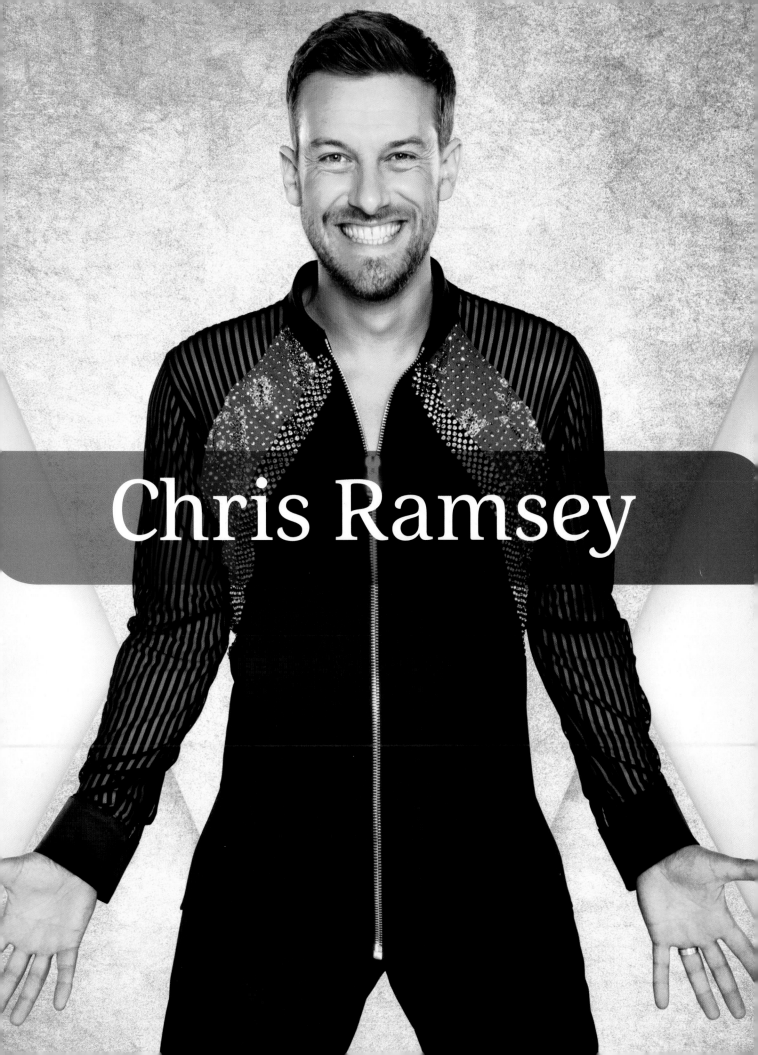

Chris Ramsey

Karen Hauer

Strictly's longest-serving female pro is paired with comedian Chris Ramsey for series 17 – and they're having plenty of fun in training.

'Chris is a bundle of energy,' she says. 'I've been laughing non-stop, to the point where I'm literally just crying. And then there's his dancing …' However, Karen is not afraid to crack the whip when the need arises.

'I'm fun, but at the same time I'm a taskmaster. I like to get in and get the work done. We're enjoying it, but it's very much focused on what he needs to learn. I need to make sure I get everything done before we go live.'

Having completely cleared his diary, Chris is able to rehearse every day, from 9 a.m. to 5 p.m., but Karen is taking care not to wear him out early on.

'I don't like to over-practice, because I don't want to exhaust him,' she says. We have a schedule that we both like, and then he goes home and spends time with his family, which is really important.'

Although Chris has never danced before, Karen says he's a fast learner. 'He's got a good energy about him and he does have rhythm. I think he will be a good dancer, once he gets the hang of it and starts feeling confident. He's never done anything like this before, so it's definitely a shock to the system for him.

'He's truly enjoying himself, but he's very disciplined as well. He tells me he has the memory of an elephant, which will be helpful. And by the second day in training we were running through the routine, which is excellent.'

Karen was born in Valencia, Venezuela, and took up dancing after moving to New York when she was eight years old. Two years later she won a scholarship to the Martha Graham School of Contemporary Dance. She studied African dance, contemporary and ballet before moving on to ballroom and Latin at 19. She went on to win numerous titles, including World Mambo Champion in 2008.

Karen's celebrity partners have included Nicky Byrne, Dave Myers and Jeremy Vine, and in 2014 she made the Final with Mark Wright. Last year, she was paired with actor Charles Venn, who shimmied all the way to the Quarter-finals.

'Charles was incredible,' she says. 'He was the most humble, hardworking and respectful partner. He got me my first 10s and it was an honour to dance with him.'

Karen had some unforgettable moments. 'The Street/Commercial dance was one of my favourite dances and I can never forget our Samba, in Blackpool, which was so much fun.'

While Karen is hoping to bag more 10s this series, she is not looking too far ahead. 'I'll take whatever comes as the weeks go by,' she says. 'I've learned over the last eight years that every week is a gift.'

Dance Off

Time to rest your dancing feet and get your thinking cap on.

Fill in the table using the clues and then jot down the first letter of each word. Then jumble those up to find something you will always find in the *Strictly* studio.

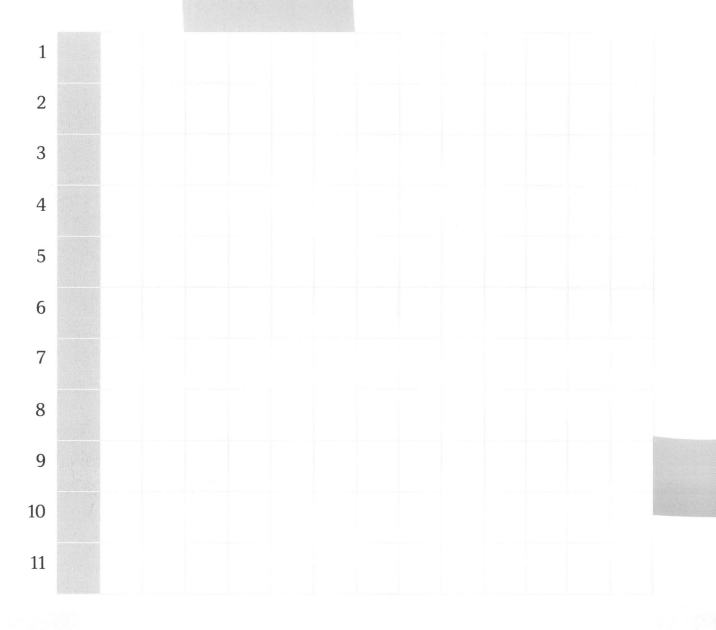

1. Model winner of series 11 (5,6)

2. The panel's most effusive judge (5,7)

3. Second Conservative MP to dance on the show (6,5)

4. Paralympian who danced with AJ Pritchard in series 16 (6,8)

5. Throughout the week the couples need to put in plenty of hours of this (8)

6. Nationality of No. 2 (7)

7. Actor and *Strictly* winner, series 6 (3,8)

8. Head judge until 2016 (3,7)

9. *Strictly*'s Spanish professional (5,7)

10. Real name of the TV judge who danced his way into the Quarter-finals in series 14 (6,6)

11. The group of dances that includes the Salsa, Samba, Paso Doble and Jive (5, 8)

Since retiring from football, in 2014, David James has turned down many celebrity shows but made an exception for *Strictly*, after talking to close friend and series six competitor Mark Foster.

'Mark told me how much he enjoyed the show and how good everyone was, so I changed my mind,' he says. 'Also, I love a challenge!

'Now I can't wait. I am really excited. I don't know what to expect and I'm sure it will be much tougher than I think but I am doing my best to prepare.'

Goalkeeper David grew up in Welwyn Garden City and started his career in the youth team at Watford. He went on to play for Liverpool, Aston Villa, Manchester United and West Ham as well as playing for England 53 times, including in the 2010 World Cup. He also modelled for Armani and H&M. Since retiring he has become a football pundit and an ambassador for the Special Olympics and Access Sports.

Although he's a fan of the show, David was surprised by the reaction to his stint on *Strictly*.

'My sister loves the show and she started rattling off who she knows and who she likes,' he says. 'Then I'm walking my dog and people are coming up and wishing me all the best. *Strictly* fans seem to be a very diverse and positive audience.'

Dad David admits his four grown up kids were shocked that he'd signed up for the *Strictly* experience.

'My kids said, 'We're surprised you're going on it.' I said: 'Does anyone want to go to the show?' They all shouted, 'Yes, yes, yes, yes.' So they're very supportive. I also have grandchildren – aged two and just two months old – and this is something that they will not be able to appreciate at the moment, but in a few years' time they'll be able to look back and go: 'That's my granddad!' I might get the first dance at their weddings, you never know.'

As a former player and coach, David is prepared for the judges and says 'I'm happy to listen to all the advice I can get! 'I know I'm not the best dancer today,' he says. 'So if I become the best dancer I've done something extraordinary. And if it means a bit of constructive criticism along the road it gets me to focus. I'm a coach and a manager and sometimes you have to tell people the way it is.'

Paired with Nadiya Bychkova, he is determined to make her proud and says that even if he doesn't have a clue to start with, 'I love to learn and if I set my mind to something, I do it. I am also ultra-competitive, I plan to go all the way. It is a competition after all.'

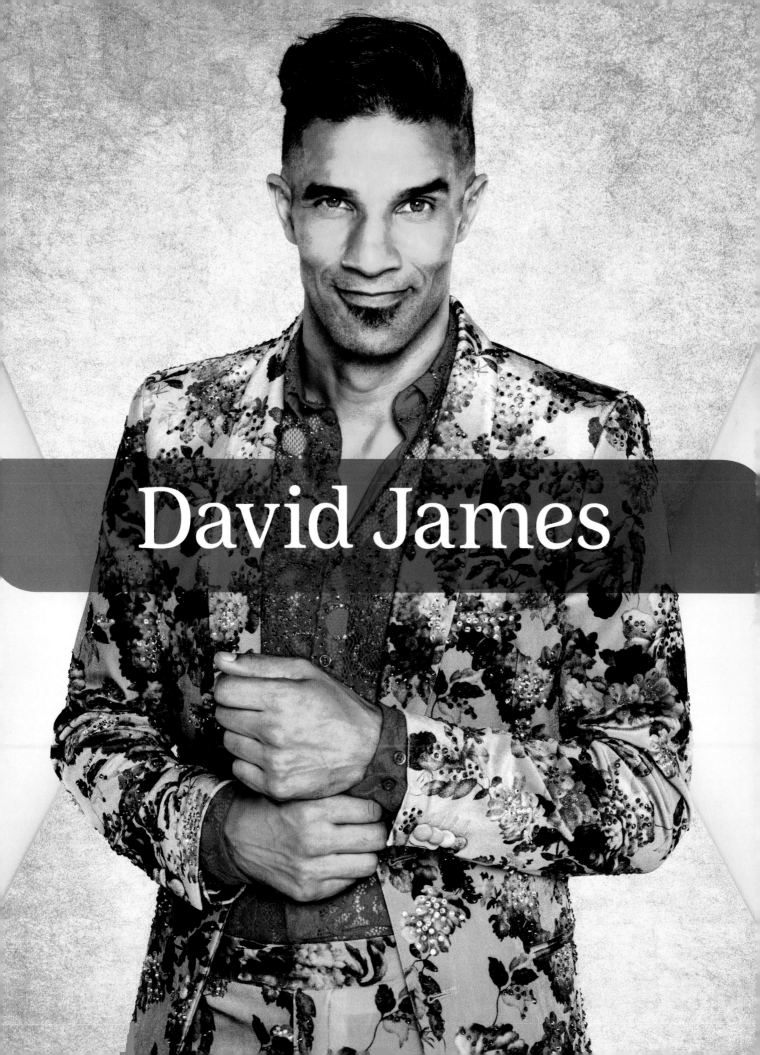

David James

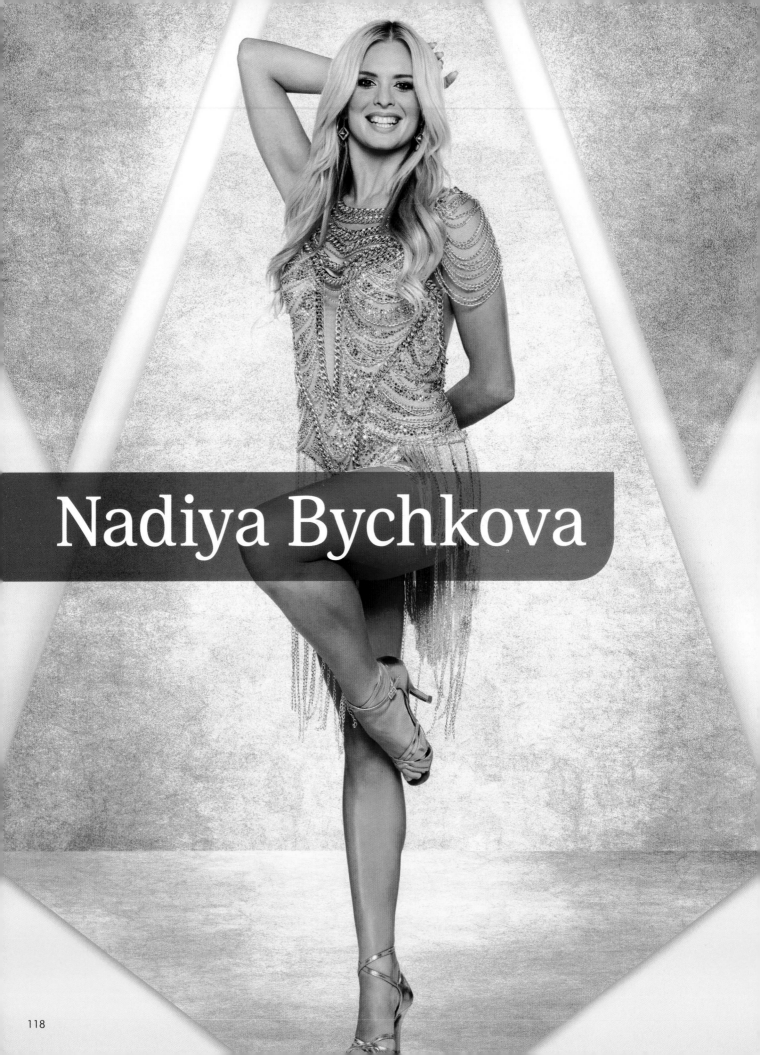

Nadiya Bychkova

Ukrainian dancer Nadiya Bychkova is hoping to hit the back of the net with goalie David James and lift the trophy. But, more importantly, she wants to make sure he savours every second.

'My strategy is to really enjoy every moment,' she says. 'Obviously, the only thing we can do is our best and then it's up to the judges and audience to decide. But for David, like all the celebrities, it's the only chance they will ever have to do *Strictly* and it's such an amazing experience. So my goal is to make sure my partner has a really nice journey, they fall in love with dancing and they just enjoy their time.'

Nadiya was born in Luhansk, Ukraine, and trained at the same Slovenian dance school as fellow pro Aljaž Škorjanec. She is a multiple-time Slovenian ballroom and Latin champion, two-time World Champion and European Champion in ballroom and Latin Ten Dance. In her first year of *Strictly* Nadiya made it to the Quarter-finals with *EastEnders* actor Davood Ghadami and last year she danced with Blue singer Lee Ryan, leaving in week three.

'Lee's a really lovely guy and very talented. I think he had a lot of potential and he didn't really have a chance to show it all.' So far, she says, England legend David James is showing potential, too. 'At six foot four inches, David is super tall, even for me, and I'm one of the tallest pros,' she says. 'I'm really pleased that he's a sportsman, so he's focused, he's ready to work. He's got his own way of learning things and he's a good student.' David has always kept physically fit and Nadiya says that helps with stamina, but only up to a point.

'He's in good condition, so he's not too tired,' she says. 'It's more of a mental challenge for him. Learning the routine and remembering the details is a whole different process from what he is used to, but he's coping well with it all.'

'People were saying he's probably more of a ballroom guy, because he's tall,' she says. 'But he's quite coordinated and he knows his body well, so I think he'll be good at Latin too. David hears the rhythm and understands the music, which is good. Now we just have to make his body understand the music.'

As well as working hard in the training room, Nadiya and David have hit it off immediately. 'I'm really enjoying it. It's really easy but focused, and I think we're going to have fun.'

Strictly Scramble

There's been a mix up in the *Strictly* production department and everybody's names have been scrambled. Can you help the team by working out the *Strictly* Hosts, Judges and a some of the pro dancers from these anagrams?

1. WICKED LUNA ANIMAL

2. CIAO NEVER PINING

3. BANKNOTE DUE

4. LADY SETS

5. WALLED BUNNIES

6. RED OWL CHAIR GROOVE

7. HERB LILY SALSA

8. JAM ART NEAR A NET

9. LION BUT ORION

10. IMBUES MOATS

Strictly Quiz

Are you a *Strictly* superfan? If you're a whizz at the Waltz and a genius at the Jive, grab a cup of Cha-cha-cha and Quickstep your way through our fun quiz.

1. Which 2018 contestant bagged five perfect scores, including the American Smooth, Charleston and Jive, before finishing as finalist?

2. Which judge got terrifying with creepy contact lenses in Halloween Week 2018?

3. Many EastEnders stars have graced the *Strictly* dance floor, but only two have bagged the trophy. Who?

4. Who was the first celebrity to leave the show in 2018?

5. Who was the first celebrity ever to perform a barefoot showdance?

6. In which dance would a 'gaucho' perform a gancho?

7. Which professional dancer has been on the show from the start?

8. Which Hall & Oates track did series 15 winner Joe McFadden perform his Showdance to?

9. After their Charleston in 2018, Craig told Faye Tozer and Giovanni Pernice he thought 'the goats were good'. Which musical was their dance track taken from?

10. Which *Strictly* pro hails from Slovenia?

11. Which actor donned a bald wig to dance as Dr Evil in series 11?

12. Which cartoon character did Kate Silverton become for her sultry series 16 Foxtrot in Movies Week?

13. Which pop star from series 15 triumphed on the 2018 Christmas Special?

14. Who was Graziano Di Primo's first *Strictly* celebrity partner?

15. Who was the first Paralympian to compete on the main show?

Graziano Di Prima

Italian dancer Graziano Di Prima joined *Strictly Come Dancing* last year and says dancing on the show and meeting the fans has been a wonderful experience.

'Moving to the UK has completely changed my life and I love it,' he says. 'This show has changed me as a person. Now I go to the theatre and the people stop me for pictures, which is great. I am doing what I know, just dancing, but it's an amazing opportunity and it's wonderful that people enjoy that.'

As part of his first year, Graziano also performed in *Strictly Come Dancing*: The Live Tour and says it proved an eye-opener for him.

'When you go into the arenas, you realize how big the show is,' he says. 'I'm used to the TV show but when you see 10,000 people in an arena, it is amazing.

I didn't expect that.

'I said to the guys, 'This is unbelievable!' And Aljaz told me every dancer feels the same. The audience is incredible.

Graziano grew up on a vineyard in a small town in Sicily and was competing at the age of six. At 17, he moved to Bologna to study dance, alongside fellow Sicilian Giovanni Pernice, and became Italian Latin Champion. He has also represented Belgium at the World Championships.

He joined *Strictly* and made his series 16 debut with DJ Vick Hope.

'It was all a new experience and a big opportunity for both of us,' he says. 'Vick was nice and she worked so hard, doing her radio show in the morning and then rehearsing for six or seven hours. But we went out on week five.'

This year, Graziano doesn't have a celebrity partner but we'll be seeing plenty of him on the *Strictly* floor, dancing up a storm in the group numbers.

'I was really lucky last year and this year, it's other people's turn to have the opportunity,' he says. 'I'm happy anyway because I'm dancing every week and I'm going to be very busy. I do my job and I love what I do, so I feel very lucky.'

Graziano says his fellow pros welcomed him with open arms last year and he is now firmly entrenched in the *Strictly* family.

Strictly isn't the only thing that has changed Graziano's life this year. During the break he proposed to girlfriend Giada Lini – on stage. 'It was my birthday and we'd just finished our solo,' he says. 'Giada was thinking that I would just say 'thank you for this experience.' But I asked her to marry me. We are getting married in Sicily I'm inviting all the *Strictly* dancers!

Nancy Xu

When new *Strictly* pro Nancy Xu got the call to confirm she was joining the show, she was in South Korea – and she was stunned.

'I was dazed and my mind was empty; it didn't sink in,' she recalls. 'But my body reacted and I got goosebumps. I'd been waiting for this moment for such a long time, and suddenly it's happened.

'I felt that something unbelievable happened to me. It's amazing. This is my dream.'

Nancy grew up in China and got the dancing bug at the age of four. 'My mum saw that whenever music played, I just jumped around. She said, "Okay, maybe she wants to learn how to dance."' Although Nancy's mum found a dance class, she wouldn't discover ballroom until she was eight.

'In China at the time, there weren't many people learning ballroom dance. I come from a very small city where some people didn't even know what a ballroom dance is. Then one professional competitor came to teach us.'

When she was just 11, Nancy moved away from home to the city of Guangzhou to attend a dancing school, and by 16, she was competing and travelling the world – including frequent stays in Norbury, southwest London.

'There were a lot of good teachers in Norbury, so we always came to the UK a month before each competition to study,' She credits her mum with steering her towards her dance success.

'When I was young, my mum always told me that if you want to do something, you have to keep going,' she says. 'You can't give up – it's really hard to fight for your dream.

Nancy says everyone has welcomed her with open arms.

'They're absolutely lovely,' she says. 'They're all so warm and welcoming. Everyone in the whole *Strictly* production team is amazing. Everyone's taken care of me.'

Now fully in the swing of the show, Nancy is loving the experience. 'Every second for me is like a dream come true and I enjoy it

Gorka Márquez

Former Finalist Gorka Márquez partnered Katie Piper last year and left in week five. But he says he found a lifelong friend.

'I loved last series, because Katie is such a special person,' he says. 'I am still in contact with her and we speak loads. For me, she's inspirational because she can always take something positive out of everything.'

Born in Bilbao, Spain, Gorka took up dancing at 12 and soon became one of the country's top talents. In 2010, he represented Spain in the World Latin Championships and two years later he reached the Semi-finals of the WDSF (World DanceSport Federation) World Cup.

Gorka's first *Strictly* partner, in series 14, was *EastEnders* star Tameka Empson, but they were sadly eliminated in week three. The following year he danced up a storm with former *X Factor*-winner Alexandra Burke, getting to Final.

While they didn't get their hands on the glittering prize, the couple racked up a record number of perfect 10s, with 32 – a feat only matched by Ashley Roberts and Pasha Kovalev last year.

This year Gorka is not paired with a celebrity but is enjoying taking centre stage in the group dances. As a new dad, he is looking forward to spending more time with Mia, his daughter with partner Gemma Atkinson.

'I will have plenty to keep me busy and it gives me the chance to spend more time with baby Mia in these precious first months.'

This year, the Spanish dancer has been watching from the sidelines and thinks there may be a few surprises to come. 'It's hard to say what their ability is at this stage, but they all look very enthusiastic, a happy bunch of people. Everyone is very nice, very positive, and very energetic. I think it is going to be a great series with diverse, different characters.'

Latin champ Gorka is also looking forward to seeing his old friend Motsi Mabuse take her chair on the judges' panel.

'When I used to compete, back in the day, I trained in Germany. She is so much fun. I think she will be great in the show.'

Answers

Which Pro is Which

1. Luba Mushtuk
2. A.J. Pritchard
3. Janette Manrara
4. Gorka Márquez
5. Amy Dowden
6. Johannes Radebe
7. Oti Mabuse
8. Kevin Clifton
9. Karen Hauer
10. Neil Jones
11. Nadiya Bychkova
12. Graziano Di Prima
13. Katya Jones
14. Anton du Beke
15. Dianne Buswell
16. Aljaž Škorjanec
17. Nancy Xu
18. Giovanni Pernice

Dance Off

1. Abbey Clancy
2. Bruno Tonioli
3. Edwina Curry
4. Lauren Steadman
5. Training
6. Italian
7. Tom Chambers
8. Len Goodman
9. Gorka Márquez
10. Robert Rinder
11. Latin American

KEY WORD:
Glitterball

Strictly Scramble

1. Claudia Winkleman
2. Giovanni Pernice
3. Anton du Beke
4. Tess Daly
5. Dianne Buswell
6. Craig Revel Horwood
7. Shirley Ballas
8. Janette Manrara
9. Bruno Tonioli
10. Motsi Mabuse

Strictly Quiz

1. Ashley Roberts
2. Shirley Ballas
3. Jill Halfpenny and Kara Tointon
4. Susannah Constantine
5. Louis Smith
6. Argentine Tango (the hook movement)
7. Anton du Beke
8. You Make My Dreams
9. The Sound of Music
10. Aljaž Škorjanec
11. Mark Benton
12. Jessica Rabbit
13. Aston Merrygold
14. Vick Hope
15. Jonnie Peacock